Polishing the "PUGS"

Polishing the "PUGS"

PUNCTUATION, USAGE,

GRAMMAR, AND

SPELLING TIPS

FOR WRITERS

KATHY IDE

UpWrite Books

ISBN 13: 978-1-4141-1031-8
ISBN 10: 1-4141-1031-6
Library of Congress Catalog Card Number: 2007903525

ENDORSEMENTS

DON'T BUY A COPY OF KATHY IDE'S PUGS!
That's right. Don't buy a copy. Buy two copies: one for yourself and one for someone you'd like to help.

Grammar/punctuation books abound by the hundreds. Kathy's offers a service that's invaluable. She cites *The Chicago Manual of Style.* Every time Kathy gives a rule or principle, she cites the *CMOS* reference.

I wonder how many people realize what an invaluable service she's offering.

I have two popular style books on my desk. Both of them make statements without backing them up. I prefer to have the backing of *CMOS* on every bit of editing I do.

Please take my advice: ***Buy at least two copies.*** Someone else will be glad you did.
—Cecil Murphey, author and coauthor of more than 100 books

Kathy Ide's PUGS manual is a result of her knowledge of the subject and thorough research. Her love for the language and for writing is evident. This resource will be a favorite for writers, editors, teachers, and everyone else who enjoys words.

—Pam Pugh, Moody Publishers

Kathy Ide's *Polishing the PUGS* is a fantastic resource. Concise, well researched, and conveniently organized. I refer to it often.

—Deborah Raney, award-winning novelist

I cannot possibly recommend Kathy's PUGS book strongly enough! I hazard to guess that 95% of the questions one has about punctuation, usage, grammar, and spelling are covered here. It's so easy to grab the book from the side of my computer, find what I'm looking for in the Table of Contents, and have an answer to my PUGS question—in *seconds*.

—Amber Ferguson, freelance author and editor

I've been writing for many years, and I've learned a lot through my writing and critique groups that I didn't pick up in my English classes. But with *Polishing the PUGS*, Kathy has put together information that I'm going to treasure with my Strunk and White.

—Gloria Clover, freelance author and editor

I have been writing, editing, and proofreading professionally since 1976. Kathy Ide's wonderful book, *Polishing the PUGS*, is worth so very much. She has addressed issues that I have not seen covered elsewhere, and I am extremely familiar with many style/grammar books. Her examples and explanations are some of the best I have encountered. I cannot recommend it enough.

—Marilyn A. Anderson, freelance editor and writer

Table of Contents

Resources xiii
Acknowledgments xv
Introduction xvii
Reference Books xxi
Ten Reasons to Polish Your "PUGS" xxiii

SECTION 1: PUNCTUATION

Apostrophes 29
    Possessives 29
    Descriptive Phrases 30
    Plurals 30
    For...sake Expressions 31
    To Replace Omitted Letters 31
    Years 31
Capitalization 33
    Family Relationships 33
    Terms of Endearment 33
    Terms of Respect 33
    Pronouns for God 33
    Regional Terms 34
    Religious Terms 35
    Titles and Headings 35
    Topographical Names 37

Small Caps 37

Colons and Semicolons 39
   Colons 39
   Semicolons in Compound Sentences 39
   Semicolons with Adverbs...40

Commas...43
   Cities and States 43
   Compound Predicates 43
   Dates..43
   Dependent vs. Independent Clauses 44
   Exclamations 44
   Interjections 45
   Introductory Phrases 45
   Introductory Yes and No 45
   "Jr." and "Sr." 45
   Multiple Adjectives...46
   Restrictive vs. Nonrestrictive Clauses 46
   Serial Commas 46

Dashes..49
   Types of Dashes...49
   Em Dash 50
   En Dash 51

Ellipses 53
   Fragmented Speech 53
   Omissions 53
   Beginning and End of Quote 53
   The Four-Dot Ellipsis 53
   Punctuation with Ellipses 54
   Spacing...54

Italics...57
   Direct Internal Discourse 57
   Citing Sources 58
   Foreign Words...58
   Letters as Letters...59
   Words as Words...59

Lists 61
   Vertical Lists after Complete Sentences...61

Vertical Lists after Introductory Phrases..61
Numbered Lists...62
Bulleted Lists...62
Numbers 65
Numerals or Words 65
Times of Day 66
Dates...67
Consistency and Flexibility..67
Periods 69
Spacing between Sentences 69
Initials 69
Run-in Quotations 69
Block Quotations 70
Omission of Period...70
Quotation Marks...73
Double and Single Quotation Marks...73
Placement with Periods and Commas..73
Placement with Colons and Semicolons 73
Placement with Question Marks and Exclamation Points..................74
Block Indents 74
Quoting Other Sources 77
Citing Sources...77
Accuracy...77
Scripture References 78
Portions of Verses 78
Bible Versions 78
Punctuation Tips...83

SECTION 2: USAGE

Commonly Misused Words...87
accept/except...87
advice/advise 87
affect/effect..87
aid/aide 88
aisle/isle..88
all ready/already 88
all together/altogether...88

altar/alter 89
any more/anymore 89
a while/awhile 89
back door/backdoor 89
back-seat/backseat 89
back up/backup 90
bad/badly 90
best seller/best-selling 91
blond/blonde 91
brake/break 91
breath/breathe 92
callous/callus 92
capital/capitol 92
car pool/carpool 93
cite/sight/site 93
clench/clinch 93
coarse/course 94
complement/compliment 94
complementary/complimentary..94
council/counsel 95
desert/dessert 95
disc/disk 95
discreet/discrete 95
elusive/illusive 96
emigrate/immigrate 96
ensure/insure 96
entitled/titled 96
every day/everyday 97
farther/further 97
fliers/flyers 97
foreword/forward 97
good/well 97
home school/homeschool 98
in to/into...98
it's/its 99
jeep/Jeep..99
lead/led 99

lightening/lightning 99
loose/lose...99
nauseated/nauseous 100
on to/onto 100
oral/verbal 100
passed/past 100
peak/peek/pique 101
personal/personnel 101
pore/pour 101
premier/premiere...101
principal/principle...102
prophecy/prophesy 102
raise/rise 102
reign/rein 103
set up/setup 103
some time/sometime/sometimes..103
stationary/stationery...104
their/there/they're..104
under way/underway 104
verses/versus 104
waist/waste 105
whiskey/whisky 105
weather/whether 105
who's/whose...105
X-ray/Xray/x-ray 105
your/you're...106

SECTION 3: GRAMMAR

Common Grammatical Mistakes...111
    among vs. between 111
    anxious vs. eager...111
    as vs. like 111
    couple vs. couple of..111
    different from vs. different than...112
    each other vs. one another..112
    fewer vs. less 112
    lay vs. lie..112

more than vs. over 113

myriad 114

reason, why, and because 114

that vs. which 115

that vs. who 115

try and vs. try to 115

was vs. were 115

Modifiers 119

Dangling Modifiers 119

Simultaneous Modifiers 120

Misplaced Modifiers 120

Pronouns 123

Pronoun/Antecedent Agreement 123

Pronouns as Subjects or Objects 125

Subject/Verb Agreement 127

Grammar Myths 129

SECTION 4: SPELLING

Commonly Misspelled Words 135

Trademarks 141

Publishers' Preferences 145

Terms for Modern Technology 147

Slang/Sounds 149

Hyphenation 151

Ages 151

Colors 151

Compound Modifiers 152

Adverb Phrases 153

Prefixes and Suffixes 154

Numbers 157

Simple Fractions 157

Mixed Fractions 157

Fractions as Compound Modifiers 157

Measurements 157

Conclusion 161

Resources

The Chicago Manual of Style. The University of Chicago Press, Chicago 60637. © 1969, 1982, 1993, 2003 by The University of Chicago.

Merriam-Webster's Collegiate® Dictionary, Eleventh Edition. Copyright © 2003 by Merriam-Webster, Inc.

Webster's New World College Dictionary, Fourth Edition. Copyright © 2002 by Wiley Publishing, Inc.

The Christian Writer's Manual of Style. Robert Hudson. Copyright © 2004 by the Zondervan Corporation.

The Associated Press Stylebook and Briefing on Media Law. Norm Goldstein, ed. Copyright © 2004 by The Associated Press, published by Basic Books/Perseus Publishing.

Merriam-Webster's Dictionary of English Usage. Merriam-Webster. Copyright © 1994 by Merriam-Webster, Inc.

Grammatically Correct: The Writer's Essential Guide to Punctuation, Spelling, Style, Usage and Grammar. Anne Stilman. Copyright © 1997 by Writer's Digest Books.

Dictionary of Problem Words and Expressions. Harry Shaw. Copyright © 1987 by McGraw-Hill Inc.

Acknowledgments

⌁

I would like to thank my editing clients—aspiring writers, established authors, commercial publishing houses, subsidy publishers, and magazines—for inspiring me to strive for excellence…and to research the appropriate rules in the industry-standard reference books.

A special thanks to my family members who patiently put up with my quirks and idiosyncrasies—like refusing to follow a truck that had an advertisement on the back with *its'* on it…and complaining that big national companies ought to be able to hire ad agencies that know when *everyday* should be spelled as two words…and muttering grammar corrections under my breath when someone on television misuses the English language…and praising the local grocery store for having express-lane signs that say "Ten Items or *Fewer.*"

Thanks also to my writing colleagues, who have peppered me with questions about punctuation, usage, grammar, and spelling, then raved about how much I knew on these subjects (apparently not realizing that I merely knew where to look up the right answers), and who affectionately dubbed me "the PUGS lady." And thanks to all the conference directors and attendees who have allowed me to speak on such a boring-sounding topic and make it fun.

Thanks to my friends who cringe whenever they write me an e-mail because they're just sure I'll notice errors in their messages…but click Send anyway.

And a deep expression of gratitude to God, my heavenly Father, who has blessed me with such wonderful and understanding friends, family members, clients, and colleagues. And to His Son, my Lord and Savior, Jesus Christ, for giving His all so that I can have assurance of eternal life in heaven with Him…whether my "PUGS" are polished or not.

Introduction

⟨ornament⟩

It was not long ago that the prevailing attitude among editors was, "This book has some problems, but the author is so talented that I'd like to buy it and work with him." Today such words are rarely heard. A book with problems is a book rejected.

—Richard Curtis, literary agent
quoted in *The Christian Communicator,* June 2001

"A book with problems is a book rejected." Can you feel the burden settling on your shoulders with that brief observation? *Not only do I have to come up with an interesting plot idea, fascinating characters with unique voices, appropriate scenes and summaries, dialogue and narrative, conflict and suspense, titillating hooks, action verbs, ways to show instead of tell, an attention-grabbing beginning and a satisfying conclusion, but I also have to worry about the mechanics? Say it isn't so!*

Wish I could. But it's true. Editors receive so many manuscripts from so many authors these days that they can afford to reject them for the most miniscule reasons. The October 2004 issue of *Write to the Heart* (newsletter of the American Christian Fiction Writers) revealed the top pet peeves of nine acquisitions editors from major Christian publishing houses. One said that her main pet peeve was "sloppy manuscripts full of grammatical errors."

Now, why would a publisher reject a perfectly good manuscript just because it has a few mechanical errors? Don't they have proofreaders and editors to fix that sort of thing? Well, yes, they do. But publishing houses have to pay editors to find all the mistakes in a manuscript before it goes to typesetting. Then they pay proofreaders to fix all the errors the editors missed. (Even then, not every mistake gets caught.)

If an acquisitions editor is reading a submission and thinking, *It's going to take hours for our editors and proofreaders to fix all the problems with this,* his next thought might be, *Maybe it's not worth it.* If the next manuscript he picks up is free of mechanical mistakes, the prudent decision would be to go with that one. Publishing is a business. Editors have to make choices that are good for business.

In addition, if an acquisitions editor notices misspelled words, incorrect punctuation, and grammar mistakes, he will begin to wonder what other details might be wrong within the manuscript. If the author didn't look up proper spelling or comma rules, perhaps she didn't do her research in other areas either.

Even if you've already had one or more manuscripts accepted for publication, you can really impress your publisher if you "polish the PUGS" before submitting your work. Your editors will be able to focus more on content if they don't have to worry about the mechanics. And the less time your proofreaders have to spend fixing the mistakes, the less money your publisher will have to spend on that part of the process...which will be one more advantage in your favor when you pitch your *next* manuscript!

In this book, I offer pointers that will help you take that terrific story of yours and polish up the "small stuff," eliminating some of the problems that could cause your great manuscript to be—heaven forbid—*rejected!*

About Me

So, who am I to be offering this kind of advice? I have been a published author since 1989. I've written books, magazine articles, play and movie scripts, short stories, curriculum, and devotionals. I've been a full-time freelance editor since 1998. I work with both fiction and nonfiction book-length manuscripts, short stories, articles, devotionals, and play scripts. I've done editing, proofreading, and critiquing for aspiring writers, established authors, publishing houses (including Moody Publishers, Thomas Nelson, Barbour/Heartsong, WinePress, and several smaller presses) as well as organizations such as CLASServices. I mentor aspiring writers, taking them from "I've never had anything published, so I don't even know if I have what it takes, but I have a passion in my heart to write and I want to learn how to do it right" to landing an agent, getting a book contract, and seeing their work in print. Several of my clients have won awards and/or become best-selling authors.

I am also the founder and coordinator of The Christian PEN: Proofreaders and Editors Network and the Christian Editor Network. And I speak at writers' conferences across the country.

I guess what first got me focused on the "picky stuff" was a course I took in transcribing court reports. See, court reports are official legal documents, usually printouts of statements made by witnesses, defendants, and prosecutors. The transcriptionist needs to make absolutely certain that the printed account of a person's testimony is clear and unmistakable. The smallest error in spelling or punctuation can alter the meaning of a sentence. After I graduated from this course, I was offered a job as an instructor. The position required, among other things, carefully proofreading students' work and catching every little mistake, as well as attending monthly meetings where the staff discussed things like when *setup* should be spelled as one word or two and when *doctor* should be capitalized and/or abbreviated.

Then again, I've always been intrigued by the way the tiniest mark of a pen or stroke of a key can make an enormous difference in meaning. I remember, when I was in elementary school, my teacher wrote this sentence on the blackboard: "The inheritance was divided equally between Tom, Dick and Harry." She asked the class how much money each person would get based on this sentence. Everyone assumed that Tom and Dick and Harry would each get one third. But they were wrong. To begin with, the absence of a comma before the "and" made "Dick and Harry" a single entity. In addition, the word *between* denotes two people or things. If the money was to be divided into more than two parts, the word *among* would have to be used. Now, perhaps the writer of this sentence *intended* for these three people to each get one third of the money. But legally, the interpretation of this sentence would result in Tom getting one half while Dick and Harry each received one quarter.

I find great amusement in noticing when sentences mean something different from what the author intended because of an error in punctuation, usage, grammar, or spelling. For instance, did you know that if you write, "My husband Derek and I went camping last week," you are implying that the man you vacationed with was only *one* of your husbands?

My familiarity with the publishing industry's reference books began when I started proof-reading for publishing houses. If something didn't look right to me, I wasn't allowed to simply change it to whatever I thought was right. If I marked a revision to the galleys, I had to make a notation in the margin stating which *Chicago Manual of Style* rule applied or what version of *Merriam-Webster's Collegiate Dictionary* I found the correct spelling in.

As you read through this book, you may get to the point where you throw your hands up and say, "Who really cares if I spell *awhile* as one word or two as long as the reader knows what I mean?" I encourage you to read the chapter on "Ten Reasons to Polish Your PUGS." If you don't want your manuscript to be confusing, embarrassing, costly, or distracting…or to remain unpublished…this book is for you!

Reference Books

There are many punctuation and grammar books on the market, but the standard used by American book publishers today is *The Chicago Manual of Style*. Some publishers have their own style guides, which may include a few exceptions to the *CMOS* rules (but you won't know that until you get hooked up with a particular house).

There are several dictionaries out there, too, and strangely enough, they don't always agree on the spellings of all words. The standard for US book publishers today is *Merriam-Webster's Collegiate Dictionary*.

Supplemental to these references, most Christian book publishers rely on *The Christian Writer's Manual of Style* for details that are not fully covered in the secular publications.

Unfortunately, these reference books sometimes contradict one another. In those cases, this is the usual order of authority:

1. The publishing house's individual style guide
2. *The Chicago Manual of Style* for punctuation and grammar
3. *Merriam-Webster's Collegiate Dictionary* for spelling and usage
4. *The Christian Writer's Manual of Style* by Robert Hudson
5. *Words into Type* by Marjorie E. Skillin et al
6. *The Elements of Style* by Strunk and White

If you write book-length manuscripts, I strongly encourage you to pick up a copy of the most recent edition of each of these books.

The Chicago Manual of Style is about a thousand pages long and can be rather confusing until you get used to it, so I will summarize here some of the common problem areas I have come across in my freelance work with authors and publishers. For each rule, I've included the abbreviation "*CMOS*," along with the section number, in case you'd like more detail on a particular subject (using the 15th edition, © 2003). I'll use "*CWMS*" when referring to *The Christian Writer's Manual of Style* (© 2004).

WHAT ABOUT ARTICLES?

If you write articles for newspapers or journalistic magazines, the standard reference books are *The Associated Press Stylebook* (© 2004) and *Webster's New World College Dictionary* (the official dictionary of the Associated Press). For religious terms, *The AP Stylebook* recommends the *Handbook of Denominations in the United States* and the *World Christian Encyclopedia*.

For Articles

I have inserted block-indented notes (like this one) wherever *The Associated Press Stylebook* ("*AP*" in the text) differs from *The Chicago Manual of Style* and when *Webster's New World College Dictionary* (for articles) differs from *Merriam-Webster's Collegiate Dictionary* (for books).

Yale's Style Guide is the standard for online writing. This book is available online at www.webstyleguide.com. The rules aren't much different, other than for special characters and some formatting.

Ten Reasons to Polish Your "PUGS"

Why should you bother learning about punctuation, usage, grammar, and spelling?

1. **PUGS errors can decrease your chance of acceptance by a publisher.**
   You may think that as long as you've got good content in your nonfiction manuscript, or a good story with lots of conflict and interesting characters in your fiction manuscript, that should be enough. And yes, content and story are very important. But no matter how good those things are, if you have too many mechanical errors, your manuscript may not go any farther than the acquisitions editor's desk.

2. **PUGS errors can cause miscommunication.**
   The example I gave in the Introduction about Tom, Dick and Harry shows how punctuation and usage can affect the meaning of a sentence. If someone wrote, "The inheritance will be divided equally between Tom, Dick and Harry," Tom would receive half while Dick and Harry split the other half. If you're Tom, that might sound pretty good. But if you're Dick or Harry, you probably won't be too happy. If you're the writer of the will, your money and possessions may be distributed in a different way than you intended.

3. **PUGS errors can cause confusion.**
   My older son, Tom, is a very busy professional, so a lot of our communication takes place via e-mail. One Sunday, I asked him what he wanted me to make for dinner that evening. His response was: "When you decide what you can say I decided this and if it's not OK that's OK." It took me a while to decipher it. And when I asked my son for permission to quote that, his response was, "Did I write that? What on earth does it mean?" Even *he* didn't know! Well, after reading that line several times, I came up with

this: "When you decide what, you can say, 'I decided this,' and if it's not OK, that's OK." Pretty confusing without the punctuation, isn't it?

4. **PUGS errors can give an unprofessional appearance to publishers and readers.**
Most acquisitions editors know a lot about proper punctuation, usage, grammar, and spelling. Most people on publishing committees know a lot about PUGS too. You don't want them looking at your manuscript and thinking, *This author has some good things to say, but she sure doesn't know a comma from a semicolon.*

Even if your manuscript has already been accepted, if your editor has to spend all her time fixing your mechanics, she won't be able to catch the deeper, more subtle nuances of your text. Besides, you won't be presenting a very polished, professional image to your publisher.

5. **PUGS errors can be embarrassing.**
A friend of mine once picked up a book at a bookstore and noticed a PUGS error on the back cover. When she reported it to our critique group, she didn't say she'd found a mistake on a book published by "XYZ Publishers." She said she found the mistake on a "Jane Doe" novel. She didn't connect the error to the publishing house, but to the author.

Many readers, especially avid ones, are familiar with the rules of punctuation, usage, grammar, and spelling. If your reader knows the rules and you don't, that's not going to make you look very good.

6. **PUGS errors may cause readers to take you and your message less seriously.**
Ireland On-Line ran an article on their Web site on November 15, 2004, with this title: "Crowe Turns Hero to Help Snake Bite Boy." The story was about actor Russell Crowe helping a boy who'd been bitten by a snake. But by spelling *snakebite* as two words, this sentence implies that Mr. Crowe helped a snake bite a boy! Now, I got a good laugh out of that. But I sure don't want those kinds of mistakes showing up in my own writing.

And take a look at this statement made in a major newspaper: "Officers found two rifles, a large bag of marijuana packaged for sale, a small scale, a bullet-proof vest and dozens of bullets in a sock." If readers are giggling about the image of all these items being found in one enormous sock, they won't be paying as much attention to the point of the article.

7. **PUGS errors can affect the sales of your book.**

   Readers who find a lot of mistakes in your book will not be as likely to recommend that book to their friends. And who knows? You may have a high school English teacher reading your book, and she just might recommend it to her students…unless there are a lot of PUGS errors in it.

8. **PUGS errors could cost you money.**

   If you decide to hire someone to edit or proofread your manuscript, and you haven't corrected your punctuation, usage, grammar, and spelling, you will be paying extra for someone else to do that for you. And how will you know if that editor is right?

9. **PUGS errors can be distracting.**

   If I'm reading a book or article, no matter how good the content or story might be, if there are too many mistakes in punctuation, usage, grammar, or spelling, it's difficult for me to get past those enough to concentrate on the book. I have been known to stop reading a book and put it back on the shelf if I find too many errors. And there are other readers like me out there.

10. **PUGS errors can give Christians and Christianity a poor reputation.**

   The world watches Christians carefully. Many people are just waiting for us to make mistakes, actually hoping we will make mistakes so they can "prove" that Christians are stupid and, therefore, Christianity is only for the uneducated and easily duped.

   Christian authors are even more closely scrutinized and criticized than the general public. Many people refuse to buy or read Christian books because they don't think ours are as well written as those published by the secular press. They consider Christian writers and publishers "inferior." And if they find errors in a Christian book, they will use those mistakes as "proof" of their point.

   Polish your PUGS so that your work reflects positively on your faith and your Lord.

Details Are Important

How much time and effort have you put into the other aspects of your writing? Is your manuscript not worth polishing? If your craft was pottery, would you go to the effort of creating a beautiful pot and then not glaze it? If you were a carpenter, would you build a coffee table and not stain and varnish it? If you made an afghan, would you not tie off the last row? If you sewed a garment, would you not finish the seams and hems?

And if you did create something without finishing it properly, would you put out your unfinished craft for sale to strangers, expecting people to pay you for it?

Professionalism Is Key

I love to sing, and my voice sounds delightful when I'm alone in my car with the radio blaring. But I wouldn't dream of asking someone to pay to hear me belt out a tune. Not without taking some serious singing lessons.

If you're writing just for family and friends, it may not matter so much whether every comma is in exactly the right place. But if you want to get your book published in today's highly competitive commercial market, you need every edge you can get. If you expect people to buy what you write, you need to take the time to learn how to do it right.

A Writer's Tools

Words and punctuation marks are the tools of a writer's trade. It is important for you to know how to use your tools properly.

That's what this book is all about. Consider it an "owner's manual" for the tools you use in your writing every day.

Section 1

Punctuation

Some people think punctuation doesn't really matter, that they should be able to put commas and other punctuation marks wherever seems right to them. But the way a sentence is punctuated can affect the meaning. And for writers who want to come across as professionals, it's important to punctuate according to accepted industry-standard guidelines.

Apostrophes

‑⁂☉

Possessives, *CMOS* #7.17–7.21, 7.27 and *CWMS* pp. 306–308 and *AP* pp. 196–198 and 326.

To form the possessive of most *singular* nouns (proper or otherwise), add an apostrophe and an *s*. Examples:

the book's success	a reader's favorite genre
Robert Burns's poems	Chris's manuscript
Kentucky's legislature	John Williams's plotline
an hour's time	a month's absence

Exception: If the word or name ends in an unpronounced *s,* use apostrophe only. Examples:

the marquis' mother	Descartes' dreams

To form the possessive of *plural* nouns ending in *s*, add an apostrophe only. Examples:

the Williamses' house	the puppies' tails
two weeks' notice	authors' rights

Use apostrophe-s if the plural term involved does not end in *s*. Examples:

women's novels	children's books

For Articles

The AP Stylebook (page 326) suggests using an apostrophe only (no extra *s*) for singular proper names ending in *s*. Examples:

Dickens' novels   Jesus' life   Xerxes' armies   Moses' law

For singular common nouns ending in s, add apostrophe-s unless the next word begins with an *s* (p. 196). Examples:

hostess's invitation   witness' story

According to *The Chicago Manual of Style* (#7.20), names that end in an *eez* sound are exceptions to this rule. Example:

Xerxes' army

The Christian Writer's Manual of Style states that the exception applies when a name has two *s* sounds in the last syllable. Examples:

Jesus'   Ramses'   Kansas'

Descriptive Phrases, *CMOS* #7.27 and *AP* p. 327

An apostrophe is not used when a modifier is "attributive"—used in a descriptive sense, as an adjective, rather than showing possession. The old rule of thumb was that if something is *for* the group or *of* the group, rather than *owned by* the group, don't use an apostrophe. However, the latest version of *CMOS* recommends retaining the apostrophe (except with proper names, such as corporate names) except when there is clearly no possessive meaning. Examples:

a teachers' college   Publishers Weekly
a writers' conference   Diners Club
writers' guidelines
a used books sale (the books don't have any possessive claim on the sale)

Plurals, *CMOS* #7.6–7.16 and *CWMS* p. 51 and *AP* pp. 190–192

Do not use an apostrophe for most plurals. Examples:

dos and don'ts   no ifs, ands, or buts
ABCs   VIPs
the 1980s   the Joneses
five Toms, four Dicks, and three Harrys
"I had to go to two DMVs to get my license renewed."

For Articles

The AP Stylebook says that "ifs, ands, or buts" and "1980s" are the preferred spellings (pp. 191–192), even though they are exceptions to *Webster's New World College Dictionary.*

Exception: To avoid confusion, pluralize single lowercase letters as well as abbreviations with two or more periods (or that have both capital and lowercase letters) by adding apostrophe-*s*. Examples:

x's and y's	a's and b's
p's and q's	M.A.'s and PhD's

For...sake Expressions, *CMOS* #7.22 and *AP* p. 326

"For...sake" expressions usually leave off the *s* when the noun ends in an *s* or an *s* sound. Examples:

for righteousness' sake   for goodness' sake   for heaven's sake

To Replace Omitted Letters, *CMOS* #7.31 and *AP* p. 328

An apostrophe replaces omitted letters in a word. Examples:

readin' and writin'
'tis the season
rock 'n' roll
ne'er-do-well

Years, *CMOS* #9.34 and *CWMS* p. 51 and *AP* p. 328

If years are abbreviated to two numerals, they should be preceded by an apostrophe. Example:

Kimberly's first novel was published in '82.

NOTE: If you're using "curly quotes," make sure the apostrophes (and single quotation marks) are curled in the right direction. Examples:

'82, not '82
'tis, not 'tis

ADD YOUR OWN

As you look up rules in *The Chicago Manual of Style, The Christian Writer's Manual of Style,* or *The Associated Press Stylebook,* you may find yourself needing to find the same rule over and over. To save yourself time, jot down here anything you think you'll need in the future. Be sure to note the appropriate section so you can check it again if needed.

My Favorite Apostrophe Rules

Reference Book:_____Rule or Page #:_____

_____

_____

_____

Reference Book:_____Rule or Page #:_____

_____

_____

_____

Reference Book:_____Rule or Page #:_____

_____

_____

_____

Capitalization

Family Relationships, *CMOS* #8.39 and *CWMS* p. 111 and *AP* pp. 91–92
   "Kinship names" (father, brother, aunt, cousin, etc.) are lowercased when used generically or when preceded by a modifier. Examples:
   my dad   the youngest mother in the group

   When used in place of the name, kinship names are capitalized. Examples:
   "I know that Mother's middle name is Janice."
   "Does Aunt Becky have a book signing on Saturday?"
   "Will her uncle Ed be at the birthday party?"
   "Hey, Dad, are we going fishing today?"

Terms of Endearment, *CMOS* #8.39 and *CWMS* p. 112
   Terms of affection (honey, dear, sweetheart) are always lowercased.

Terms of Respect, *CMOS* #8.35
   Honorific titles are capitalized. But general terms of respect are not. Examples:
   His/Her/Your Majesty   His/Her/Your Excellency   His/Her/Your Honor
   my lord   my lady   sir   ma'am

Pronouns for God, *CMOS* #8.102 and *CWMS* pp. 169–170
   The newest edition of *The Chicago Manual of Style* states that pronouns referring to God or Jesus are not capitalized. (Note: This is different from the 14th edition.) Their reasoning is that these pronouns are lowercased "in most English translations of the Bible."

The Christian Writer's Manual of Style says, "The capitalization of pronouns referring to persons of the Trinity has been a matter of debate for many decades.... Impassioned arguments have been offered up on both sides of the question." They then cite Zondervan's policy, which is: "In most cases, lowercase the deity pronoun."

The reasons given by Zondervan are as follows. (Note: These are excerpts. For a more complete explanation, see pages 169–170 of *The Christian Writer's Manual of Style*.)

"Many religious publishers and most general publishers have adopted the lowercase style, in large part to conform to the styles of the most commonly used versions of the Bible (the KJV, the NIV, and the RSV). Because capitalizing the deity pronoun was the predominant style in the late nineteenth- and early twentieth-century publishing, it gives a book, at best, a dated, Victorian feel, and at worst, an aura of irrelevance to modern readers.

"Contrary to popular opinion, capitalization is not used in English as a way to confer respect. (We capitalize both God and Satan, Churchill and Hitler.) Capitalization is largely used in English to distinguish specific things from general. Jesus is no more specific, in that sense, than Peter, and both should therefore be referred to as *he*."

CWMS adds, "There are some situations in which the capitalization of deity pronouns is preferred; for instance, in books that have a deliberately old-fashioned tone or when the author quotes extensively from a Bible version that uses the capitalized style."

Here are my personal suggestions:

1. If writing for a specific publisher, find out their preference and use that. If you have a strong preference that differs from the publisher's, ask if they'll allow it.
2. Or use your own preference, but be consistent throughout the book.

TIP: If you choose to capitalize pronouns for deity, do *not* capitalize *who, whom,* or *whose.* But *do* capitalize *You, Your, Yours, Me, My,* and *Mine.* (See *CWMS* p. 170.)

For Articles

The Associated Press Stylebook (p. 214) says to lowercase pronouns referring to the deity.

Regional Terms, *CMOS* #8.48–8.50 and *CWMS* p. 111

Regional terms that are considered proper names should be capitalized. Adjectives and nouns are not.

<u>Examples of capitalized terms:</u>
Central America, the Orient, Eastern culture, Middle East(ern), North/South Pole, the Pole, Eastern/Western/Northern/Southern Hemisphere, the Southwest/Northwest, Upper Michigan, the East/West, Western world, West Coast (US), the Continent (Europe), an Oriental, the Midwest (US), the East/North/South/West

<u>Examples of lowercased terms:</u>
central Europe, eastern, easterner, eastern seaboard (US), the equator, northern Africa, polar regions, the south of France, oriental culture

For Articles

See *The AP Stylebook,* pages 73–74, for a list of capitalized regional terms.

Religious Terms, *CMOS* #8.111, 8.115–8.117 and *CWMS* pp. 113–132
For a comprehensive list of what religious terms should be capitalized, see *The Christian Writer's Manual of Style.* For example, while *Bible* and *Scripture* (nouns) are capitalized, *biblical* and *scriptural* (adjectives) are not. Similarly, you would capitalize "the Almighty" (noun) but not "almighty God" (adjective).

For Articles

The AP Stylebook has a list of religious terms on page 214.

Titles and Headings, *CMOS* #8.167–170 and *CWMS* p. 106
For titles of books, chapters, songs, poems, etc. and headings/subheadings, capitalize:
    the first and last words of the title
    the first word following a colon or a dash
    all nouns, pronouns, verbs, adjectives, and adverbs
    subordinate conjunctions (*when, if, as, so, that*).
Lowercase:
    articles (*a, an, the*)
    prepositions (*through, up, down, on,* etc.)
    coordinate conjunctions (*and, but, or, nor, for*)
    the words *to* and *as.*

NOTE: *CMOS*-14 recommended capitalizing *to* when used in a verb phrase. *CMOS*-15 says that *to* should always be lowercase.

<u>Examples:</u>
Four Theories concerning the Gospel according to Matthew
Looking Up Directions, Writing Them Down, and Typing Them Out
    (Note: *up, down,* and *out* are used as adverbs here, not prepositions)
Talking on Your Cell Phone in a Writers' Conference Workshop

For Articles

Per *The Associated Press Stylebook* (p. 55), for titles of books, computer games, movies, operas, plays, poems, songs, TV programs, lectures, speeches, and works of art:

Capitalize the principal words, including prepositions and conjunctions of four or more letters. Capitalize a word with fewer than four letters if it is the first or last word in a title.

Hyphenated Compounds in Titles, *CMOS* #8.169–8.170 and *CWMS* p. 45

The simple rule of capitalizing hyphenated phrases is to only capitalize the first word (unless any subsequent word is a proper name). Examples:
    "Faith-building Verses by Eighteenth-century Poets"
    "The All-Christian Church Makes Non-Bible-believing Visitors Uncomfortable"

However, *CMOS* prefers the more "traditional" (and more complex) rules:

* Always capitalize the first word.
* Capitalize all other words except articles (*a, an, the*), prepositions (*in, on, over, up, down, through*), or coordinating conjunctions (*and, but, or, nor, for*). Example: "Hard-and-Fast Rules for Writers"
* If the first part of the word is a prefix that could not stand alone (*anti, pre,* etc.), lowercase the second part of the word (unless it is a proper name). Example: "A Non-Christian's Guide to Post-resurrection Philosophies"

Lowercase the second element in a spelled-out number (*twenty-one,* etc.).
    "Lolita's Twenty-first Birthday Party"
    "A Two-thirds Majority of Non-English-Speaking Representatives"

Topographical Names, *CMOS* #8.57–8.58

Names of mountains, rivers, oceans, and islands are capitalized. When a generic term is used descriptively rather than as part of the name, or if it is used alone, it is lowercased. Examples:

the Hudson River valley, the valley of the Mississippi, the California desert,
the Kansas prairie, the Indian peninsula, the Hawaiian Islands, the island of Hawaii

NOTE: You would write "along the Pacific coast" for, say, a drive along the beach, but "Pacific Coast" if you were referring to the actual region designated as such.

Small Caps, *CMOS* #15.41, 15.44 and *CWMS* pp. 41, 45–46, 55

A.M. and P.M.

CMOS-14 and the original *CWMS* recommended using small caps with periods for A.M. and P.M. But *CMOS*-15 recommends full capitals without periods (AM and PM). *CMOS*-15 states that small caps without periods (AM and PM) or lowercase with periods (a.m. and p.m.) are acceptable. The new *CWMS* (p. 17) prefers the latter. (Just make sure you're consistent throughout your manuscript.)

B.C. and A.D.

The same situation holds true here. The *CMOS*-14 and the original *CWMS* recommended small caps with periods (A.D. and B.C.), but *CMOS*-15 and the new *CWMS* suggest full capitals without periods (AD and BC).

NOTE: AD is placed before the date; BC after. Examples:

3000 BC   AD 62

For Articles

The AP Stylebook suggests:
  lowercase with periods for a.m. and p.m. (page 192)
  all caps with periods for A.D. and B.C. (page 6)

Abbreviations for Scripture Translations

The original *CWMS* suggested using small caps for abbreviations of Scripture translations (KJV, NASB, etc.). The new version advocates full caps (NIV, NKJV).

ADD YOUR OWN

My Favorite Capitalization Rules

Reference Book:_____Rule or Page #:_____

_____

_____

_____

Reference Book:_____Rule or Page #:_____

_____

_____

_____

Reference Book:_____Rule or Page #:_____

_____

_____

_____

Reference Book:_____Rule or Page #:_____

_____

_____

_____

Colons and Semicolons

Colons, *CMOS* #6.63 and *CWMS* pp. 148–149 and *AP* p. 328

A colon introduces something (or a series of things) that illustrates or amplifies what is written before the colon. Example:

The panel consisted of three agents: Ned Aloof, Terry Friendly, and Mel Charming.

Capitalization with Colons, *CMOS* #6.64–6.66 and *CWMS* p. 148 and *AP* p. 328

The first word following a colon is lowercased unless (a) the first word after the colon is a proper noun, (b) the colon introduces two or more related sentences, (c) the colon announces a definition, or (d) the colon precedes a speech in dialogue or a quotation. Examples:

Latisha had two choices: Should she try to write a steamy romance novel? Or should she go for a self-help book about punctuation addiction?

Kevin: My book has already been printed.
Timothy: Then you can't correct the error until the second printing.

Matthew 6:24 makes this clear: "You cannot serve both God and Money."

Semicolons in Compound Sentences, *CMOS* #6.57 and *CWMS* p. 370 and *AP* p. 336

A semicolon should be used between two parts of a compound sentence when they are *not* connected by a conjunction. Example:

"She removed the novel from the shelf; in its place she put a book on prayer."

If there is a conjunction, use a comma (unless one or both of the independent clauses contain a comma). Examples:

"She removed the novel from the shelf, and in its place she put a book on prayer."

"Sarah wanted to approach the Tyndale editor at lunch; but, since that table filled up before she arrived, she ended up sitting with the Multnomah editor."

Many publishers prefer that independent clauses be separated into individual sentences. Example:

"She removed the novel from the shelf. In its place she put a book on prayer."

Semicolons with Adverbs, *CMOS* #6.58 and *CWMS* p. 371 and *AP* p. 336

The words *then, however, thus, hence, indeed, accordingly, besides,* and *therefore* are adverbs; therefore, there should be a semicolon before them when they're used as transitions between parts of a compound sentence. (The preceding sentence is the example.)

ADD YOUR OWN

My Favorite Capitalization Rules

Reference Book:_____Rule or Page #:_____

_____

_____

_____

Reference Book:_____Rule or Page #:_____

_____

_____

_____

Reference Book:_____Rule or Page #:_____

_____

_____

_____

Reference Book:_____Rule or Page #:_____

_____

_____

_____

Reference Book:_____Rule or Page #:_____

_____

_____

_____

Reference Book:_____Rule or Page #:_____

_____

_____

_____

Commas

Cities and States, *CMOS* #15.31 and *AP* p. 235

States, when spelled out or when the older abbreviation format is used, are surrounded by commas when they follow the name of a city. Commas may be omitted with the newer (two capital letters) format. Example:

"Zondervan is in Grand Rapids, Mich., and Moody is based in Chicago, Illinois, but Karen has lived in Bedford CT for years."

Compound Predicates, *CMOS* #6.34 and *CWMS* p. 150

A comma should not be used between the parts of a "compound predicate" (two or more verbs having the same subject).

"Kate took Gail to a writers' conference and talked her into signing up for two more."

Dates, *CMOS* #6.46

Dates in text include a comma only if the month and then the date precede the year.

"On October 10, 1980, Donita submitted her fourth book in the series."

When using only the month and year (or date, then month, then year), do not use a comma.

"Copyright October 1980"

"On 6 October 1924 Angelina wrote her first poem."

Dependent vs. Independent Clauses

Dependent Clauses, CMOS #6.35–36 and CWMS p. 152 and AP p. 329
A dependent clause (that is, one that cannot be omitted without changing the meaning of the sentence) should be followed by a comma when it precedes a main clause.
"After she read Rene Gutteridge's book, Linda felt motivated to write a novel too."

If the dependent clause follows a main clause, it should not be preceded by a comma if it is essential to the meaning of the sentence.
"Patty rejoiced when her manuscript was accepted by the publisher."

If the dependent clause is supplementary or parenthetical, it should be preceded by a comma.
"Lynette didn't speak to the editor, because she was afraid she'd stutter."

Independent Clauses, CMOS #6.32 and CWMS p. 152 and AP p. 329
An independent clause is a part of a sentence that could stand on its own as a complete sentence. If you put two of these together and join them with a conjunction (*and, but, or,* etc.), separate them with a comma. Examples:
"Carl mailed the proposal, but he forgot to include a self-addressed envelope."
"Darlene looked startled by the acceptance, and Spencer nearly fainted on the couch."

Exception: Short clauses don't need a comma.
"Heather designed the cover and Cheryl wrote the text."

Exception to the exception: Use the comma if there's a chance the meaning of the sentence could be misconstrued. Example:
"Everyone was surprised by the arrival of the principal, and several students who had been gossiping in the hall rushed into the classroom."
(Without the comma, a reader might read, "Everyone was surprised by the arrival of the principal and several students…" By the time the sentence is completed, the meaning is clear. But you don't want to make your reader go back and reread.)

Exclamations, *CMOS #6.27 and CWMS p. 153 and AP p. 332*
Use a comma after exclamatory *oh* or *ah* if a slight pause is intended. Examples:
"Oh, what a frightening cover!" Lana said when she saw James Scott Bell's latest novel.
"Ah, how charming!" Rachel said when she finished Deb Raney's sequel.

No comma after vocative *O* or *Oh*. Examples:

    "O mighty king!"   "Oh great warrior!"

"Oh yes," "Oh yeah," and "Ah yes" are written without a comma. When spoken like a single word, "Yes sir" and "No ma'am" may be written without a comma. If "sir" is used in direct address, use the comma. Example:

    "No, sir, I disagree."

Interjections, *CMOS* #5.192–197

Commas should be used to set off interjections. Examples:

    "Well, I don't like to brag, but my last book sold twenty copies."
    "Why, I can't even imagine that kind of success."
    "Hey, I meant twenty thousand copies."

Introductory Phrases, *CMOS* #6.25 and *AP* p. 329

An adverbial or participial phrase at the beginning of a sentence is followed by a comma. Examples:

    "Blessed by the morning's devotional, Bethany sent an e-mail to the author."
    "If your manuscript gets rejected, send it somewhere else."

Exception: A single word or very short phrase does not require a comma. However, if misreading is a possibility, or comprehension could be slowed, put the comma in. Example:

    "In typesetting, the publisher will insert the en dash."
    (You wouldn't want your reader to read, "In typesetting the publisher,…")

Introductory Yes and No, *CMOS* #6.29 and *AP* p. 330

When starting a sentence with *yes* or *no,* use a comma if a slight pause is intended.

    "Yes, I included a self-addressed, stamped envelope," Nick stated.
    "No, I haven't finished polishing my manuscript," Elizabeth said with a sigh.
    "No way. Did you really make the CBA best seller list?" asked Margie.

"Jr." and "Sr.", *CMOS* #15.19 and *CWMS* p. 154 and *AP* p. 134

Jr. and *Sr.,* as well as numerals like *II* or *3rd,* following a person's name should not be separated with a comma. Examples:

    Harold Harrison Sr.   Charles Winchester III

Multiple Adjectives, *CMOS* #6.39 and *CWMS* p. 152 and *AP* p. 329

If a noun is preceded by two (or more) adjectives that could be joined by *and* without changing the meaning, the adjectives should be separated by a comma. Example:

"DiAnn proved to be a faithful, sincere friend."

If the noun and the adjective right before it are considered a unit, no comma should be used.

"Samantha has had many intriguing *romance novels* published."

"Jillian rejected traditional *royalty publishing* in favor of a small *subsidy publisher*."

Restrictive vs. Nonrestrictive Clauses, *CMOS* #6.31 and *CWMS* p. 151 and *AP* p. 330

A word or phrase that is "nonrestrictive" (restates a noun or pronoun in different words without changing or adding to the meaning of the sentence) is set off by commas. Example:

"My husband, Richard, got a promotion."

(My husband's name is Richard, so either "my husband" or "Richard" could be eliminated from this sentence without changing its meaning.)

If, however, the word or phrase has a "restrictive" function (identifies the noun more specifically), it is not set off by commas. Example:

"My son Michael is eight years younger than his brother."

(I have more than one son, which is obvious from the context of the sentence. "Michael" identifies which of my sons is being referred to in this sentence.)

If you're not sure whether more than one thing exists, leave out the commas. Example:

"Carmen Leal's book *The Twenty-Third Psalm for Caregivers* is a tremendous blessing for anyone who is taking care of an ill or elderly relative."

(However, in this case, you should do a little research and find out if the author has written more than one book.)

Serial Commas, *CMOS* #6.19 and *CWMS* p. 151

In a series of three or more elements, separate the elements by commas. When a conjunction joins the last two elements in a series, use a comma before the conjunction. (*The Chicago Manual of Style* strongly recommends this "widely practiced usage.") Example:

"Frank, Greg, and Ken argued over whether to give their wives copy paper, printing cartridges, or writers' conference tuition for their birthdays."

For Articles

The AP Stylebook (page 328) recommends leaving out the comma before *and* (or another conjunction) in a series, unless doing so would cause confusion or ambiguity.

ADD YOUR OWN

My Favorite Comma Rules

Reference Book:_____Rule or Page #:_____

_____

_____

_____

Reference Book:_____Rule or Page #:_____

_____

_____

_____

Reference Book:_____Rule or Page #:_____

_____

_____

_____

Reference Book:_____Rule or Page #:_____

_____

_____

_____

Reference Book:_____Rule or Page #:_____

_____

_____

_____

Reference Book:_____Rule or Page #:_____

_____

_____

_____

Reference Book:_____Rule or Page #:_____

_____

_____

_____

Dashes

Types of Dashes

Two kinds of dashes are most often used in manuscripts:
em dash —
en dash – (half the length of an em dash but longer than a hyphen)

TIP: Some word processors can automatically convert hyphens to en dashes and em dashes. [In MS Word, see Tools/AutoCorrect/AutoFormat. Put a checkmark in "Symbol characters (--) with symbols (—)."] With this feature checked, follow these steps:

To make an en dash (–), type a letter or word, insert a space, then type a hyphen, then type the next letter or word, followed by a space.

To make an em dash (—), type a word (*do not* insert a space), then type a double hyphen, then type the next letter or word followed by a space.

Alternately, you can insert an en or em dash using "Insert/Symbols," then clicking on the "Special Characters" tab. This menu also lists keyboard shortcuts you can use.

Another way to do it (if you have MS-Word) is to hold down the Ctrl key and hit the hyphen on the numeric keypad for an en dash, or hold down the Ctrl and Alt keys and hit the hyphen on the numeric keypad for an em dash.

If You Can't Type Dashes, CMOS #6.80

A hyphen may be used in place of an en dash, and a double hyphen can be typed to represent an em dash.

> **NOTE:** *The Chicago Manual of Style* says there should be no space before or after either dash.

For Articles

The AP Stylebook (p. 330) says there *should* be a space before and a space after an em dash. The en dash is not used in articles. (Use a hyphen instead.)

> **NOTE:** *Yale's Style Guide* (see www.webstyleguide.com) recommends not using en or em dashes for Web writing since they are not supported in standard HTML text.

Em Dash

Break in Thought, CMOS #6.90–6.91and *CWMS* pp. 165–166 and *AP* p. 330

Use an em dash to denote a sudden break in thought that causes an abrupt change in sentence structure. Example:

"Will he—can he—obtain the endorsements he needs?"

An em dash is used in dialogue to indicate that one person's speech has been interrupted by another. If an em dash is used at the end of quoted material to indicate an interruption, insert a comma before the speaker attribution. Example:

"Honey," Mark began, "I was thinking—"

"About what?" Andrea interrupted.

"Well, I thought it could be helpful if I—," he mumbled, but Andrea cut him off again.

For narrative that breaks up a line of dialogue, both em dashes go outside the quotation marks. Example:

"Someday I'll get published, but"—her voice cracked—"it won't be any time soon."

Complementary Element, CMOS #6.88 and *CWMS* pp. 165–166

A word or phrase that is added to or inserted in a sentence for purposes of defining, enumerating, amplifying, or explaining may be set off by em dashes.

"Charlotte could forgive every insult but one—the snub by her coauthor."

"Three novelists—Francine Rivers, Angela Elwell Hunt, and Karen Kingsbury—have most influenced my own writing."

Don't Get Carried Away, CMOS #6.87 and *CWMS* p. 167

If a comma, parentheses, or colon would do just as well, use one of them rather than a dash. Never have more than one dash—or pair of dashes—in a sentence.

En Dash

En Dash with Numbers, CMOS #6.83 and *CWMS* p. 168

The en dash is used for connecting inclusive numbers, including dates, time, or reference numbers. It signifies "up to and including" or "through." Examples:

1981–1982

pages 31–33

Daniel 13:3–15

Multiple-Word Compound Adjectives, CMOS #6.85 and *CWMS* p. 168

Use an en dash in a compound adjective when one of the parts is an open compound or when two or more parts are open or hyphenated compounds. Examples:

the post–World War II years   a hospital–nursing home connection

Universities, CMOS #6.86

Use an en dash to link a city name to the name of a university that has multiple campuses.

The University of California–Fullerton

ADD YOUR OWN

My Favorite Dash Rules

Reference Book:_____Rule or Page #:_____

_____

_____

_____

Reference Book:_____Rule or Page #:_____

_____

_____

_____

Reference Book:_____Rule or Page #:_____

_____

_____

_____

Reference Book:_____Rule or Page #:_____

_____

_____

_____

Ellipses

Fragmented Speech, *CMOS* #11.45 and *CWMS* p. 191 and *AP* pp. 331–332

Use ellipsis points to indicate faltering or fragmented speech, often accompanied by confusion, insecurity, distress, or uncertainty.

"I...or rather, we...yes, *we* made a terrible mistake," Emily cried.

"These awful rejection letters...what should I do about them?" Naomi moaned.

Like dashes, frequent use of ellipses for this purpose is discouraged.

Omissions, *CMOS* #11.51 and *CWMS* p. 192 and *AP* pp. 331–332

Use ellipsis points to show that part of a sentence or passage has purposely been left out. This is most often used when quoting Scripture. Example:

Ephesians 3:20–21 says, "Now to him who is able to do immeasurably more than all we ask or imagine,...to him be glory in the church...throughout all generations."

Beginning and End of Quote, *CMOS* #11.54 and *CWMS* p. 192 and *AP* p. 331

In most cases, ellipsis points should not be placed before or after a Scripture verse or other quoted passage, since it is assumed that the quote was taken out of a larger context (unless the quote is a sentence fragment or might be confusing to the reader).

Introductory words such as *And, Or, For, Therefore, But,* and *Verily* may be omitted.

The Four-Dot Ellipsis, *CMOS* #11.57 and *CWMS* p. 192 and *AP* p. 332

A four-dot ellipsis (a period followed by a three-dot ellipsis) indicates an omission between two quoted sentences when that omission does not make those sentences grammatically incomplete. Example:

"Though I have all faith…but have not love, I am nothing.… Love never fails" (1 Corinthians 13:2, 8 NKJV).

Punctuation with Ellipses, *CMOS* #11.58 and *CWMS* p. 36

A comma, colon, semicolon, question mark, or exclamation point may be retained before or after the ellipsis if it helps clarify the meaning of the sentence.

"For he spoke,…he commanded, and it stood firm" (Psalm 33:9 ESV).

Spacing, *CMOS* #11.51 and *CWMS* p. 193 and *AP* p. 332

In typesetting, ellipsis points are separated from each other and from the text by "3-to-em spaces." To type an ellipsis in a manuscript, use three dots with a space between each (. . .).

Put a space before and after an ellipsis used in the middle of a sentence. Example:
"You could come in for a cup of coffee . . . if you take your shoes off first," Dana said.

If an ellipsis comes at the beginning or end of a quote, do not insert a space between the ellipsis and the quotation mark. Examples:
"Well . . ."
". . . whether you like it or not."

For Articles

The AP Stylebook allows for the thin space between ellipsis dots that most computers convert to when three periods are typed in a row (when that "Auto Correct" option is selected). However, a full space should be inserted before and after an ellipsis (except when in conjunction with an open or close quotation mark).

ADD YOUR OWN

My Favorite Ellipses Rules

Reference Book:_____Rule or Page #:_____

_____

_____

_____

Reference Book:_____Rule or Page #:_____

_____

_____

_____

Reference Book:_____Rule or Page #:_____

_____

_____

_____

Reference Book:_____Rule or Page #:_____

_____

_____

_____

Italics

Direct Internal Discourse (unspoken thoughts)

According to the 14th edition of *CMOS* (#10.43) and *AP* pp. 334–335, direct thoughts, imagined dialogue, and other interior monologue, when expressed in first-person form, are typed in italics. Examples:

Tracey looked at him in despair and thought, *Now what have I done?*

Lucinda clearly heard God's direction. *Go apologize to Claudia. Now!*

The 15th edition of *CMOS* (#11.47) and *CWMS* p. 243 state that interior discourses *may* be enclosed in quotation marks or straight type, according to the writer's preference. Examples:

"I don't care what he thinks," Veronica thought. "I'll never see him again."

Lord, Sandra prayed, I wish I'd listened to You.

The reasoning behind this change is that long stretches of italics can be difficult to read and that italics can be mistaken for emphasis. However, long sections of direct, first-person internal dialogue should be used sparingly anyway, regardless of how it is punctuated (with the exception of books that are written from first-person point of view).

Italicizing direct internal dialogue has been the standard for a long time, and replacing this convention with quotation marks could be jarring for readers who are used to the italics. Therefore, not all publishers are making this change…at least not right away.

Indirect Thought, *CMOS* #11.48

Interior thought that is indirect or paraphrased should not be in italics or quotes. Example:

> "Melody told herself she didn't mind having to cut 21,000 words from her manuscript."

Citing Sources, *CMOS* #8.172, 8.196, 17.49 and *CWMS* pp. 244–245

Large works that can be subdivided into smaller components should be italicized (such as book titles—including subtitles—album titles, periodical names, movie titles, play titles, names of TV programs). Smaller, stand-alone components should be in quotation marks (chapter titles, song titles, section titles, short story titles, poem titles, titles of episodes). Example:

> After watching the movie *Chicago,* Bill tried to read *The Hobbit,* but the tune to "All That Jazz" kept playing in his mind, so he decided to study a *Reader's Digest* article titled "Getting Stuck Tunes Out of Your Head."

For Articles

The AP Stylebook (pp. 55–56) says that all composition titles (including books, movies, plays, poems, songs, TV programs, lectures, speeches, and works of art) should be in quotation marks (not italics).

Exceptions: the Bible, and books that are primarily catalogs of reference materials (such as almanacs, dictionaries, encyclopedias, and handbooks).

Foreign Words, *CMOS* #7.51 and *CWMS* pp. 242–243

Foreign words and phrases should be in italics if they will probably be unfamiliar to most readers. If it's a fairly common word, check Webster's Collegiate to see if the word has been adopted into English. If so, don't italicize.

For Articles

The AP Stylebook (p. 99) says that foreign words that are not universally understood should be placed in quotation marks (with an explanation of the meaning).

Letters as Letters, *CMOS* #7.63

Italicize individual letters of the alphabet (unless used in a common expression). Examples:

> the letter *s*
> a capital *M*
> He signed the paperwork with an *X*.
> Mississippi is spelled with four *i*'s and four *s*'s.
> Mind your p's and q's
> Dot the i's and cross the t's

Words as Words, *CMOS* #7.62 and *CWMS* p. 244 and *AP* p. 277

Italicize words used as words, or phrases used as phrases. Examples:

> "The word *love* has many meanings, Amber," Rob said.
> "Is that why the phrase *I love you* is so hard for you to say?" she retorted.

ADD YOUR OWN

My Favorite Italics Rules

Reference Book:_____Rule or Page #:_____

_____

_____

_____

Reference Book:_____Rule or Page #:_____

_____

_____

_____

Reference Book:_____Rule or Page #:_____

_____

_____

_____

Reference Book:_____Rule or Page #:_____

_____

_____

_____

Reference Book:_____Rule or Page #:_____

_____

_____

_____

Reference Book:_____Rule or Page #:_____

_____

_____

_____

Lists

Vertical Lists after Complete Sentences *CMOS* #6.127–128 and *CWMS* pp. 286–288

The best way to introduce a vertical list is with a complete sentence, followed by a colon. Items in the list have no closing punctuation unless they are complete sentences. If items run over one line, the subsequent lines are indented. Example:

A book proposal should include the following:

> synopsis
> author bio and publishing credits
> market comparison
> title page with the byline centered under the title, and the author's name and contact information in the lower-left corner
> three sample chapters

Vertical Lists after Introductory Phrases *CMOS* #6.129 and *CWMS* p. 288

If a list completes a sentence that begins with an introductory phrase, don't use a colon after the introductory phrase. If any of the phrases or sentences in the list have internal punctuation, semicolons may be used at the end of each item. Each item begins with a lowercase letter. A period should follow the final item. Example:

You can reduce redundancy in your writing by

> avoiding repetition;
> stating what you mean in the fewest words possible;

omitting unnecessary adverbs and adjectives;
eliminating weak words like *actually, basically, definitely, extremely, so,* and *very.*

Numbered Lists *CMOS* #6.127 and *CWMS* p. 287

If the items are numbered, a period follows each numeral and every item begins with a capital letter. Runover lines are aligned with the first word following the numeral. Example:

Here are some of the most common mistakes beginning writers make:

1. Flowery writing
2. Overuse of adjectives and adverbs
3. Long sentences and paragraphs
4. Lack of transitions
5. Repetition/redundancy
6. Poor mechanics, including typos, errors in grammar and punctuation, misspelled words, and misused words

Bulleted Lists *CMOS* #6.127 and *CWMS* p. 288

Bullets can improve clarity and ease of readability in unnumbered lists, but they can lose their impact if used too frequently. Example:

To format your manuscript for a publisher, follow these guidelines:

*   Use wide margins, at least one inch.
*   Double-space all text. Indent new paragraphs five spaces. Do not leave extra space between paragraphs.
*   Use Courier, Courier New, Times, or Times New Roman, 12 point.
*   For special emphasis, use *italics*, not ALL CAPS or **bold**.
*   Never bind your pages in any way.

NOTE: Bullets are not recommended for Web writing, per *Yale's Style Guide* (see www.webstyleguide.com), since they are not supported in standard HTML text.

ADD YOUR OWN

My Favorite List Rules

Reference Book:_____Rule or Page #:_____

_____

_____

_____

Reference Book:_____Rule or Page #:_____

_____

_____

_____

Reference Book:_____Rule or Page #:_____

_____

_____

_____

Reference Book:_____Rule or Page #:_____

_____

_____

_____

Numbers

⁓⧸⧹◉

Numerals or Words, *CMOS* #9.3, 9.14, 9.16, 9.19 and *CWMS* p. 282

Spell out whole numbers one through one hundred, round numbers (hundreds, thousands, millions), numbers referring to someone's age, and any number beginning a sentence. Use numerals for all other numbers. Examples:

"We need fifty thousand copies of the book by May," Megan insisted.

"If three more people sign up," Sally said, "I will need 121 copies of the handout."

"Nineteen eighty-seven was the year they met."

"Nathan was fifty-three years old when he sold his first novel."

Always use numerals with percents. Spell out *percent*, and never use a hyphen. (This rule applies to articles as well. See *AP* pages 180–181.) Example:

"Only 2 percent of the local population own a Bible," Debbie announced.

Measurements (distance, length, area, height, etc.) are treated according to the general numbers rule. Example:

"Stanley is six feet one (or, more colloquially, six foot one)."

Measurements with a combination of numbers and simple fractions may be spelled out if they're short, but better to write them with numerals. Example:

"I'm exactly 5 feet 4½ inches tall."

For Articles

The AP Stylebook (p. 73) suggests using numerals and spelling out *inches, feet, yards,* etc. Hyphenate adjective phrases when followed by nouns. Examples:

Larry is 6 feet 5 inches tall (but "the 5-foot-6-inch man")
The basketball team signed a 7-footer.
The book is 6 inches wide, 9 inches tall and 2 inches thick.
The rug is 9 feet by 12 feet (but "the 9-by-12 rug")

Apostrophes and quotation marks (5'6") are only used in very technical contexts.

Times of Day, *CMOS* #9.41–9.42 and *CWMS* p. 388

Spell out times of day in even, half, and quarter hours. Examples:

| seven o'clock | eleven thirty | quarter of four | five fifteen |

Use numerals (with zeros for even hours) to emphasize the exact time. Examples:

"The workshop starts promptly at 2:30 this afternoon," Courtney said.
"If we leave now, we can catch the 6:20 train," Stacy said breathlessly.
"Turn the clocks back at precisely 2:00," Susan reminded everyone.
"She woke up at five o'clock, but the meeting didn't start until half past seven, so she lounged around until six thirty, then missed her seven-thirty appointment."

Dates, *CMOS* #9.35 and *AP* p. 68

Use numerals for dates (Example: December 4), even though it could be pronounced as an ordinal (December 4th).

When a day is mentioned without the month or year, the number is usually spelled out. Example:

> "On November 5, Deirdre received her first book advance. By the seventeenth, she was lounging on the beach in Maui."

Consistency and Flexibility, *CMOS* #9.7 and *CWMS* p. 282

If several references to numbers appear in the same paragraph, you may treat them all alike to simplify the reader's comprehension. However, with similar items in a single sentence or paragraph, you may use both numerals and words.

> "I've compiled a collection of short stories—one with 115 words, five with about 75 words each, and ten with only 1 or 2 paragraphs."
> "Between 1,950 and 2,000 people attended the writers' conference."

For Articles

The AP Stylebook says to stick to the above rule even in a series (p. 177).
"The family had 10 dogs, six cats, and 14 hamsters."

ADD YOUR OWN

My Favorite Numbers Rules

Reference Book:_____Rule or Page #:_____

_____

_____

_____

Reference Book:_____Rule or Page #:_____

_____

_____

_____

Reference Book:_____Rule or Page #:_____

_____

_____

_____

Reference Book:_____Rule or Page #:_____

_____

_____

_____

Reference Book:_____Rule or Page #:_____

_____

_____

_____

Periods

Spacing between Sentences, *CMOS* #6.11 and *CWMS* p. 378 and *AP* p. 334

One space, not two, follows a period (or any other punctuation mark) that ends a sentence.

Initials, *CMOS* #8.6, 15.12 and *CWMS* p. 12

Initials standing for given names are followed by a period and a space.

    Examples: J. R. R. Tolkien   C. S. Lewis

For Articles

The AP Stylebook (p. 122) says to use periods but *no space* for initials in a name (to ensure that the first two initials don't get split onto two lines).

Run-in Quotations, *CMOS* #11.79, 11.80 and *CWMS* p. 137

After a "run-in quotation" (a quote that is included in the running text of a paragraph), cite the source after the closing quotation mark, followed by a period or question mark. Examples:

Jesus said, "I am the way and the truth and the life" (John 14:6).

Was Paul advocating slavery when he wrote, "Slaves, obey your earthly masters in everything" (Colossians 3:22)?

If the quote is in the middle of a sentence, the reference is inserted immediately following the ending quotation mark, before any necessary punctuation.

> When Jesus said, "I am the way and the truth and the life" (John 14:6), His followers did not fully comprehend what He meant.

When a quotation comes at the end of a sentence, and it is a question or exclamation, that punctuation stays inside the quotation marks. Add a period after the closing parentheses. Example:

> When the Lord asked Cain where Abel was, Cain replied, "Am I my brother's keeper?" (Genesis 4:9 KJV).

Block Quotations, *CMOS* #11.81 and *CWMS* pp. 348–349

Cite the source of a block quotation in parentheses after the quotation (in the same-size type). Put the opening parenthesis *after* the final punctuation mark of the quote. No punctuation goes after the source. Example:

> Then I saw a new heaven and a new earth, for the old heaven and the old earth had disappeared. And the sea was also gone. (Revelation 21:1 NLT)

Omission of Period, *CMOS* #6.15 and *CWMS* p. 220

No period goes chapter titles, headings, subheads, etc. (unless they are immediately followed by text within the same paragraph).

ADD YOUR OWN

My Favorite Period Rules

Reference Book:_____Rule or Page #:_____

_____

_____

_____

Reference Book:_____Rule or Page #:_____

_____

_____

_____

Reference Book:_____Rule or Page #:_____

_____

_____

_____

Reference Book:_____Rule or Page #:_____

_____

_____

_____

Reference Book:_____Rule or Page #:_____

_____

_____

_____

Quotation Marks

—⁂—

Double and Single Quotation Marks, *CMOS* #11.33 and *CWMS* p. 344 and *AP* pp. 334–336

Use double quotation marks for short quotes within the text (called a "run-in quotation"). Example:

Jesus said, "Blessed are the poor in spirit" (Matthew 5:3 NRSV).

Use single quotation marks for quotes inside quotes. Example:

"And He said to them, 'Follow Me, and I will make you fishers of men'" (Matthew 4:19 NASB).

NOTE: In typesetting, the publisher will insert a "hair space" between a single quotation mark and a double quotation mark.

Placement with Periods and Commas, *CMOS* #6.8 and *CWMS* pp. 344–345 and *AP* p. 336

Closing quotation marks always come *after* a comma or period. Example:

ACFW held workshops on "Characterization," "Point of View," and "Floating Body Parts."

Placement with Colons and Semicolons, *CMOS* #6.9 and *CWMS* pp. 344–345

Closing quotation marks always come *before* a colon or semicolon. Example:

He wrote a poem called "When I First Saw Your Crooked Nose"; his girlfriend was unimpressed.

For Articles

The AP Stylebook (p. 336) says that semicolons should go within the quotation marks only when they apply to the quoted matter.

Placement with Question Marks and Exclamation Points, *CMOS* #6.9 and *CWMS* pp. 344–345 and *AP* p. 336

Placement of question marks and exclamation points depends on whether the punctuation is part of the sentence as a whole or part of the quotation. Examples:

Bob cried, "Did that acquisitions editor even read my proposal?"

Jerry angrily replied, "He sure didn't read mine!"

They have no basis on which to say, "We don't use this kind of material"!

What gives them the right to claim, "Your work doesn't suit our needs"?

Block Indents, *CMOS* #11.23–27 and *CWMS* p. 345

Whether to set off a quotation or include it in the text is usually determined by its length. According to *The Chicago Manual of Style*, quoted matter that consists of more than one paragraph is set off from the text; shorter quotations are run into the text. *The Christian Writer's Manual of Style* recommends block indents for more than eight typed lines. Some publishers' guidelines set the cutoff at four typed lines.

Block-indented quotes should be double-spaced, indented only on the left, with an extra blank line above and below the quote.

If the text following a block quotation is a continuation of the paragraph that introduces the quotation, it begins flush left. Otherwise, use paragraph indentation.

Block quotations do not begin or end with quotation marks. Only use quotation marks if they appear in the original text. (See *CMOS* #11.35 and *CWMS* p. 38.) Example:

"For I know the plans I have for you," declares the Lord, "plans to prosper you and not to harm you, plans to give you hope and a future." (Jeremiah 29:11)

ADD YOUR OWN

My Favorite Quotation Mark Rules

Reference Book:_____Rule or Page #:_____

_____

_____

_____

Reference Book:_____Rule or Page #:_____

_____

_____

_____

Reference Book:_____Rule or Page #:_____

_____

_____

_____

Reference Book:_____Rule or Page #:_____

_____

_____

_____

Quoting Other Sources

~℘℧℗

Citing Sources, *CMOS* #16.1 and *CWMS* pp. 375–378

For reasons of ethics, copyright law, and courtesy to readers, always identify the sources of direct quotations as well as any facts, statistics, or opinions not universally known or easily verified.

There are several styles of documentation, including footnotes, endnotes, and bibliography. (See *CMOS* chapter 16 for details.)

It is the author's responsibility (not the publisher's) to research and verify the proper sources and to request written permission to quote (if not covered under Fair Use or Public Domain).

Accuracy, *CMOS* #11.8–10, 16–17 and *CWMS* pp. 348, 351–352

All direct quotations (including Scripture verses) must be reprinted *exactly* as in the original, not only the wording but the spelling, capitalization, and internal punctuation of the original, *except*:

1. Single quotation marks may be changed to double, and double to single, as the situation warrants.
2. Commas or periods outside the closing quotation mark may be moved inside.
3. The initial letter may be changed to a capital or a lowercase letter (depending on whether the quote makes a complete thought).
4. The final punctuation mark in the original quotation may be omitted or changed to suit the format of the sentence in which it is quoted, and punctuation marks may be omitted where ellipsis points are used.
5. In a passage quoted from a modern book, journal, or newspaper, an obvious typographical error may be corrected. (Leave archaic spellings the same.)

6. Words that are italicized in Scripture should not be italicized when quoted.

7. The words *Lord* and *God* should not be written in cap-and-small-cap style (LORD and GOD), even if printed that way in the original text. (*Exception:* Zondervan, the publisher of the New International Version, prefers that the cap/small-cap format be used for Old Testament uses of LORD.)

8. The King James Version capitalizes the first letter of the first word of each verse, regardless of whether the word begins a new sentence or not. Do not follow this when quoting the KJV. Capitalize only proper names, the first word of a sentence, and the first word of what is meant to be a direct quotation.

Scripture References, *CMOS* #9.30 and *CWMS* p. 359

Scripture references are given in numerals only, not spelled out. Chapter and verse are separated by a colon, with no space following it. Examples:

Acts 27:1   Genesis 47:12

At the ends of block quotations of Scripture, the references may be spelled out or abbreviated at the author's/editor's discretion, but the same format should be used consistently throughout the manuscript. (See *The Christian Writer's Manual of Style* for a list of the appropriate abbreviations.) Either of the following formats may be used:

I am persuaded that neither death nor life,...nor height nor depth,...shall be able to separate us from the love of God. (Rom. 8:38–39 NKJV)

...nor any other created thing, shall be able to separate us from the love of God which is in Christ Jesus our Lord.

—Romans 8:37–39 NKJV

Portions of Verses, *CWMS* p. 359

Don't add a letter (a, b, c, etc.) to the verse number to indicate that only a portion of a verse is being quoted. The context usually makes this clear. You could use a letter if several parts of a verse are being examined individually and successively, or if you're writing a scholarly, academic work. But this practice is not recommended for popular or trade books.

Bible Versions, *CMOS* #17.248 and *CWMS* p. 358

For every Scripture verse you quote, you must identify which Bible version you are citing. Example:

"Make a joyful noise unto the Lord, all ye lands" (Psalm 100:1 KJV).

You may indicate in the front of the manuscript which version(s) you used. (See the Scripture copyright page at the front of this book.) If only one was used, or one was used predominantly, and you identified it at the beginning, there is no need to identify the version in the text after each quote. If multiple versions are used, identify only the alternate versions.

NOTE: If you really want to impress your publisher, include complete copyright notices for each Bible version you used in the front matter of your manuscript.

ADD YOUR OWN

My Favorite Source-Quoting Rules

Reference Book:_____Rule or Page #:_____

_____

_____

_____

Reference Book:_____Rule or Page #:_____

_____

_____

_____

Reference Book:_____Rule or Page #:_____

_____

_____

_____

Reference Book:_____Rule or Page #:_____

_____

_____

_____

Reference Book:_____Rule or Page #:_____

_____

_____

_____

Reference Book:_____Rule or Page #:_____

_____

_____

_____

Reference Book:_____Rule or Page #:_____

_____

_____

_____

ADD YOUR OWN MISCELLANEOUS PUNCTUATION RULES

Reference Book:_____Rule or Page #:_____

_____

_____

_____

Reference Book:_____Rule or Page #:_____

_____

_____

_____

Reference Book:_____Rule or Page #:_____

_____

_____

_____

Reference Book:_____Rule or Page #:_____

_____

_____

_____

Reference Book:_____Rule or Page #:_____

_____

_____

_____

Reference Book:_____Rule or Page #:_____

_____

_____

_____

Reference Book:_____Rule or Page #:_____

_____

_____

_____

Reference Book:_____Rule or Page #:_____

_____

_____

_____

Punctuation Tips

Let me add two "rules of thumb" regarding punctuation.

1. Some punctuation should be used sparingly.
Avoid overusing exclamation marks. If your dialogue or narrative conveys the idea that a remark is shouted or a comment is extraordinary, you don't need to beat the reader over the head by adding an exclamation mark as well.

Avoid long chunks of italicized internal monologue. (Avoid lots of short lines of italicized direct thought as well.)

Don't use too many semicolons. Most of the time, replacing a semicolon with either a period or a comma will make your text read more smoothly.

Don't overuse ellipses or dashes. A pause in speech may be indicated with narrative beats instead. Example:
"Stop." The young woman giggled. "That tickles."

2. Be consistent.
If you've checked all the reference books and you're still not sure about something, consistency is the best line of defense. Choose the way you're going to do something, and do it that way throughout the manuscript.

Pay special attention to the use of "straight" or "curly" quotation marks, single quotation marks, and apostrophes. Since many word processing programs have the option to automatically convert "straight" marks to "curly" ones, you should proofread your work very carefully to make sure you've been consistent throughout the manuscript.

> **NOTE:** When writing for the Web, do not use "smart quotes" (the curly ones). Stick with the straight quotes. (See *Yale's Style Guide,* available at www.webstyleguide.com.) "Smart quotes" are not supported in standard HTML text

3. When in doubt, look it up.

If you're uncertain about how to punctuate a sentence, get out your copy of *The Chicago Manual of Style* and take the time to look up the rule.

Don't drive yourself crazy doing this while you're writing your first draft (or even your second or third or fourth). But before you send your manuscript to an editor or publisher, make sure every comma, semicolon, colon, and dash is exactly where it should be. Most writing techniques are subjective—once you learn them, it's up to you to determine how best to apply them to your work. But mechanics like punctuation are objective. The rules are the rules, and you bend or break them at your own risk.

Section 2

Usage

Many words in the English language are spelled differently when used in different contexts, with different meanings, or as different parts of speech. Some words may be hyphenated, or spelled as two words, depending on how they're used in a sentence.

Unfortunately, even professionally published books sometimes contain usage errors. A writer friend of mine recently noticed, on the back cover of a novel, a slogan that read something like "Christian fiction at it's best!" But "it's" is the abbreviation for "it is" or "it has." In this context, the word should have been spelled "its," without an apostrophe.

Not long ago, a well-known fast-food chain had billboards that advertised 49-cent hamburgers "everyday!" But "everyday," when spelled as one word, is an *adjective,* which means it must modify a noun (as in "an everyday occurrence"). When referring to when this sale was in effect, the wording should have been "every day" (the adjective *every* modifying the noun *day*).

Here are the words I see misused most often in the manuscripts I edit (and sometimes in the published books I read). They're listed alphabetically to make them easier to find.

Commonly Misused Words

accept/except

accept (always a verb): to receive, agree with, or say yes to
"Bethany House did not *accept* Carol's proposal."

except (verb): to omit, exempt, or exclude
"Joe was *excepted* from the list of those invited."
except (preposition): other than
"Everyone *except* Nanette had the wrong answer."

advice/advise

advice (noun): a suggestion or recommendation
"Cec gave me excellent *advice* about publishing my book."

advise (verb): to suggest or recommend
"Frani *advised* me to strengthen the conflict in my romance novel."

affect/effect

affect (always a verb, except for one use as a noun in psychology): to influence or cause a response
"This article will *affect* the reader's thinking."
affect (verb): to assume, to be given to, or to pretend
"Deborah *affected* a silly manner of speaking."

effect (noun): result or accomplishment
"What was the *effect* of this appeal for money?"
effect (verb): to cause or bring about
"The new manager will *effect* major changes in our sales methods."
effects (plural noun): goods or property
"The deceased man's *effects* were willed to charity."

aid/aide

aid (verb): to provide something useful or necessary
"One nurse can *aid* several patients during one shift."
aid (noun):
a subsidy granted for a specific purpose ("financial aid")
the act of helping, or help given ("providing aid," as in money or supplies)
something by which assistance is given ("an aid to understanding")

aide (noun): a person who acts as an assistant
"The *aide* helped the teacher hand out tests to the students."

aisle/isle

aisle (noun): passage
"We met in the grocery store *aisle*."

isle (noun): island
"We spent our honeymoon on a tropical *isle*."

all ready/already

all ready (adjective phrase): completely ready
"I am *all ready* to be published."

already (adverb): previously
"My book has *already* sold a thousand copies."

all together/altogether

all together (adverb phrase): in a group
"Let's sing this *all together* now."

altogether (adverb): wholly, completely
"The Lord is *altogether* holy."

altar/alter

altar (noun): a table or platform used in a church service
"The new bride and groom prayed together at the *altar*."

alter (verb): to change
"Roxanne hoped his outburst wouldn't *alter* their friendship in any way."

any more/anymore

any more (adjective phrase): any additional
"I don't want to hear *any more* backtalk from you!" hollered Cindy.

anymore (adverb): any longer
"I don't want to listen to you *anymore*," cried Randi.

a while/awhile

a while (noun): a period of time
"Marilyn spent *a while* editing her manuscript."

awhile (adverb): *for* a period of time
"Mallory asked me to stay *awhile*."

back door/backdoor

back door (noun)
"Tony pounded on Jim's *back door*."

backdoor (adjective): indirect or devious
"She suspected the men were involved in some kind of *backdoor* operation."

back-seat/backseat

back-seat (adjective)
"Terrence was a *back-seat* driver."

backseat (noun)
"Henry found a wad of gum on the *backseat*."

For Articles

Per *Webster's New World College Dictionary*, spell as two words (*back seat*) when used as a noun to mean "a secondary or inconspicuous position."
"Food takes a *back seat* to romance when you're in love."

back up/backup

back up (verb): to move into a position behind, or to make a copy of
"Don't *back up*," the waitress said, balancing the tray of food.
"I *back up* my computer files every day."

backup (noun): a copy of computer data
"I make a *backup* of my computer files every day."
backup (adjective): serving as a substitute or support
"Wendy decided she needed a *backup* plan."

bad/badly

bad is an adjective. In addition to the obvious definitions, it can mean suffering pain or distress. Example:
"I felt *bad* yesterday." (I experienced a condition that could be described as *suffering pain or distress*.)
bad can also mean sorrowful or sorry. Example:
"Marion felt *bad* about mailing her manuscript." (*Sad* or *sorrowful* describes the *condition* she experienced.)

badly (adverb) means in a bad manner. Example:
"He played piano *badly*." (*Badly* modifies the verb *played*; it describes *how* he played.)
badly can also mean to a great or intense degree. Example:
"If you want something *badly* enough, you'll work hard to get it." (*Badly* describes the verb *want*; it defines *how much* you want.)

The rule of thumb here is to consider whether the word describes the noun or the verb. For example, if you said, "Donna looked *bad*," you are describing how this *person* (noun) appeared to you. If you said, "Donna looked *badly*," you would be referring to the way in which she visually *observed* things (verb). (Perhaps Donna was looking for Easter eggs and missed some that weren't very well hidden.)

If you said, "Daryl smelled *bad*," you'd be describing your perception of this *person* (noun). If you said, "Daryl smelled *badly*," you'd be referring to a lack in his ability to smell.

best seller/best-selling

best seller (noun): a book that has sold more copies than most

best-selling (adjective): having sold more copies than most

NOTE: Never one word, *bestseller*

blond/blonde

blond (noun): a boy or man with blond hair
  "Sven, a muscular *blond*, strode the beach as if he owned it."
blond (adjective): of a golden, light auburn, or pale yellowish brown color
  "Ted shook the water out of his thick mane of *blond* hair."
blond (adjective): having blond hair (when used of a boy or man)
  "Rick was a *blond* man."

blonde is the feminine version of *blond* for both noun and adjective. Examples:
  "Ursula loved being a platinum *blonde*." (noun)
  "Virginia dried her long *blonde* hair with a sandy beach towel." (adjective)

For Articles

The AP Stylebook (p. 31) suggests using *blond* for males and for all adjectives (male or female), using *blonde* only when referring to females (noun).

brake/break

brake (noun): the pedal that slows the car
brake (verb): to reduce speed
  "To *brake* the vehicle, press on the *brake* pedal."

break (verb): to separate, fracture, or destroy
  "Why did I have to *break* my wrist now? I was planning to *break* up with my boyfriend tonight."

break (noun): condition produced by breaking, place where a break occurred, or interruption

"The *break* in the storm gave Sharon a chance to walk outside for the first time since she suffered that ankle *break.*"

breath/breathe

breath (always a noun) refers to the inhalation/exhalation of air.
"Tamara's *breath* was frozen in the cold air."
breath (noun) can also mean a slight indication or suggestion.
"The faintest *breath* of a scandal."

breathe (always a verb): to inhale or exhale air
"If you *breathe* deeply you will feel better."
breathe (verb): to feel free of restraint
"Martha needed room to *breathe.*"
breathe (verb): to permit the passage of air
"This fabric really *breathes.*"
breathe (verb): to utter or express
"Don't *breathe* a word," Kay begged.

callous/callus

callous or *calloused* (adjective): having calluses, or feeling no emotion or sympathy
"The suspect's *calloused* hands revealed an occupation involving physical labor."
"The reporter was a cold, *callous* man."
callous (verb): to make callous
"A childhood of abuse had *calloused* her to the needs of others."

callus (noun): a hard, thickened area on skin or bark
"The *calluses* on his hands reminded Shannon of a farmer she once dated."
callus (verb): to cause calluses to form
"The physical labor *callused* his fingertips and palms."

NOTE: mucous/mucus follows the same rule.

capital/capitol

capital (noun): money or possessions; a column; a city serving as a seat of government
"I leaned against the *capital* outside the bank, thinking about making a *capital* investment before moving to the *capital* of Iowa."

capital (adjective): punishable by death
    "Murder is a *capital* offense."
capital (adjective): chief in importance or influence
    "Professional editing is of *capital* importance."
capital (adjective): excellent
    "That was a *capital* book."
capital (adjective): not lowercased
    "That word is spelled with a *capital M*."

A *capitol* is a building, or group of buildings, where government functions are carried out. (When capitalized, it refers to the building where Congress meets in Washington.)
    "*Capitol* Hill" refers to the legislative branch of the US government.

car pool/carpool

car pool (noun): an arrangement in which a group of people commute together by car, or the group entering into such an arrangement

carpool (verb): to participate in a car pool

cite/sight/site

cite (verb): to recall, remind, mention, or specify
    "Pam *cited* Jeremiah 29:11 as her life verse."

sight (noun): eyesight, vision, or outlook
    "Out of *sight*, out of mind," Kayla said.
    "The *sight* of Janet's face left him breathless."
sight (noun) can be negative, meaning eyesore, mess, or monstrosity.
    "Rochelle's teenage daughter's room was a *sight*."
sight (noun) can also be positive.
    "Tiffany was a *sight* for sore eyes."

site (noun): place, location, situation, scene, or locale
    "The burial *site* was at Rose Hills Mortuary."

clench/clinch

clench (verb): to set or close tightly (NOTE: *Clench* is a "transitive verb," which means it requires an object, such as hands, fingers, jaws, or teeth.)
    "Melissa *clenched* her teeth when Myra *clenched* her fist."

clinch (verb): to settle, to make final or irrefutable, or to secure conclusively (NOTE: *Clinch* is most often used for the securing of an agreement, argument, or verdict.)
"Jeanette's evidence *clinched* the argument."
clinch (verb): to hold an opponent in close quarters (a boxing term)
clinch (noun): an act or instance of clinching in boxing, or an embrace

coarse/course

coarse (adjective): not fine
"*coarse* cloth"   "*coarse* language"

course (noun): a path, a customary procedure, or part of a meal
"in due *course*"   "of *course*"
"collision *course*"   "correspondence *course*"   "golf *course*"
course (verb): to pursue or move swiftly
"Airplanes *coursed* across the sky above her apartment every day, ruining the mood for writing romantic song lyrics."
"Hot blood *coursed* through Brenda's veins as she wrote her suspense novel."

complement/compliment

complement (noun): something that completes
"This book contains a full *complement* of screenwriting techniques."
complement (verb): to complete
"That jewelry *complements* Kristin's dress."
"The two coauthors *complement* each other with their different abilities."

compliment (noun): flattery or praise
"Arlene enjoyed the *compliment* Elaine paid her."

complementary/complimentary

complementary (adjective): relating to one of a pair of contrasting items
"*Complementary* colors appear directly across from each other on the color wheel."
complementary (adjective): mutually supplying each other's lack
"Steak and seafood are *complementary* dishes for the menu."

complimentary (adjective): expressing or containing a compliment
"Kathy Tyers's latest novel received many *complimentary* reviews."
complimentary (adjective): given as a courtesy or favor
"A slice of pie is *complimentary* with your meal."

council/counsel

council (noun): an assembly/meeting or an advisory or legislative group
   "city *council*"

counsel (noun): advice, or a lawyer or consultant
   "Tracie gave me good *counsel* when she suggested I hire legal *counsel*."
counsel (verb): to advise or consult
   "June *counseled* with her agent before signing the book contract."

desert/dessert

desert (noun): an arid region
   "While roaming in the *desert*, Kelly lost her way." (pronounced "DEH-zert")
deserts (noun): a deserved reward or punishment
   "Tim got his just *deserts*." (pronounced "di-ZERTS")
desert (adjective): arid
   "Diana landed on a *desert* island." (pronounced "DEH-zert")
desert (adjective): uninhabited
   "Barbara landed on a *deserted* island." (pronounced "di-ZERT-ed")
desert (verb): to withdraw or leave, usually without the intent to return
   "Do not *desert* your post now." (pronounced "di-ZERT")

dessert (noun): a sweet pastry, or the final course of a meal
   "My grandmother always eats *dessert* first." (pronounced "di-ZERT")

disc/disk

disc (noun) should be used for *compact disc (CD)*, *digital video disc (DVD)*, *disc brakes*, *disc jockey*, and *laser disc*.

disk (noun):
   the seemingly flat figure of a celestial body ("solar *disk*")
   round, flat anatomical structure ("slipped *disk*")
   the central part of a flower head
   round, flat plate coated with a magnetic substance on which computer data is stored ("hard *disk*" or "floppy *disk*")

discreet/discrete

discreet (adjective): prudent, cautious, careful, trustworthy, or circumspect
   "Never one to gossip, Rebecca kept a *discreet* silence."

discrete (adjective): separate, distinct, apart, or detached
   "This question consists of six *discrete* parts."

elusive/illusive

elusive (adjective): difficult to grasp, isolate, or identify
   "Her novel contained so many *elusive* concepts I had difficulty following the plot."
   "The *elusive* criminal led the search party farther into the woods."

illusive (adjective): based on or producing illusion; deceptive
   "The murderer's *illusive* clues took the detective on several wild goose chases."

Memory Device: *elusive* is the adjective form of the verb *elude* (meaning avoid, escape).
                   illusive is the adjective form of *illusion* (meaning deceiving, misleading).

emigrate/immigrate

emigrate (verb): to leave a country to live somewhere else

immigrate (verb): to come into a country to live there

ensure/insure

ensure (verb): to assure, to secure, to make something certain or sure
   "Jennifer wanted to *ensure* that her manuscript was received by the publisher."

insure (verb): to provide or obtain insurance on or for, or to contract to give or take insurance
   "Allstate *insured* the property against theft and vandalism, but not terrorism."

NOTE: Webster's Collegiate states that *ensure* and *insure* are somewhat interchangeable. However, *ensure* tends to imply a guarantee (as in, "His agent *ensured* the legality of the contract"), while *insure* stresses the taking of necessary measures beforehand ("Careful planning should *insure* the success of your book signing").

entitled/titled

entitled (verb): to give a title to, or to furnish with grounds for claiming
   "This ticket *entitles* the bearer to one free book."

titled (verb): to designate or call by a title
   "Cindy Woodsmall's first novel, *titled When the Heart Cries,* is on the best sellers list."

every day/everyday

every day is a combination of an adjective and a noun, synonymous with "each day."
"Daisy wrote two thousand words *every day.*"

everyday is an adjective, which means it describes a noun.
"For Josh, writing was an *everyday* activity."

farther/further

farther (adverb): at a greater distance (referring to a measurable distance or space)
"The ball traveled ten yards *farther.*"

further (adverb): to a greater degree or extent
"Brendan wanted to discuss the problem *further.*"

fliers/flyers

fliers are people who fly.
flyers are pieces of paper.

Memory Device: *I* can fly on a plane; there's an *i* in *fliers.*
Flyers only fly if you fold them into *y*-shaped paper airplanes.

For Articles

According to *The AP Stylebook* (p. 96):
fliers are aviators or handbills.
flyers refers to some trains and buses (for example, The Western Flyer).

foreword/forward

foreword (noun): a page or two of comments at the beginning of a book

forward (adverb, adjective): in front, or toward the front
forward (noun): a player on a sports team who tries to score points in a game

good/well

good (adjective): favorable, suitable, advantageous, agreeable

"a *good* time"   "a *good* book"
good (adjective): free from infirmity or sorrow
  "I feel *good*."
  "He felt *good* about presenting his proposal at the conference."

In the above instances, *feel* is used as a "linking verb," which makes the word *good* an adjective modifying the pronoun.

good is sometimes used as an adverb in colloquial speech. (Examples: "You wrote that scene real *good*" or "I'm doing *good*, thanks.") This usage should not appear in narrative writing.

well (adjective): in good health
  "I feel *well*."
well (adverb): ably
  "The cast performed *well*."

home school/homeschool
home school (noun): a school taught in someone's home
  "All of Lynn's children graduated from *home school*."

homeschool (verb): to teach school at home
  "Alberta *homeschooled* her first child for two years; she *homeschools* the second one now; she plans on *homeschooling* the youngest one through high school."

NOTE: *Homeschooler* (noun) is one word. Example:
  "Steve found a support group for *homeschoolers*."

in to/into
in to (*in* is an adverb; *to* is a preposition)
  "Judith turned her manuscript *in to* the publisher."

into (preposition) indicates movement or direction to an interior location, or a change of condition or form.
  "Sonja transformed her rough draft *into* a publishable manuscript."

NOTE: If you wrote, "As long as I turn my proposal *into* the right editor at the conference, I will definitely get published," you would be implying that you had plans to somehow put your proposal inside the editor (an interior location) or to make your proposal *become* an editor (a change of condition or form). In either case, you probably won't get published.

it's/its

it's is the contraction of "it is" or "it has."
"*It's* clear to me now how *it's* become such a common mistake."

its is possessive
"Wanda knew the manuscript had *its* faults, but she didn't know how to fix them."

NOTE: There is no such word as *its'*.

jeep/Jeep

jeep is lowercased when referring to the military vehicle.

Jeep is capitalized when referring to the make of four-wheel-drive civilian vehicle.

lead/led

lead (noun, long *e* sound): direction or example
"Follow my *lead*."
lead (noun, short *e* sound): a heavy, soft metal

led (past-tense verb): to show the way, or to conduct or escort
"The experiment *led* Brock to believe that *lead* was the best material to use."

lightening/lightning

lightening (verb): becoming lighter; illuminating, shining, brightening; making something brighter; reducing in weight or quantity
"The acceptance from the publisher went a long way toward *lightening* Veronica's mood."
"Sybil's boss refused to consider *lightening* her duties after the accident."

lightning (noun/adjective): the flash of light in the sky that usually accompanies thunder
"The *lightning* bolt lit up the night sky for an instant."

loose/lose

loose (adjective): not tightly bound (rhymes with "goose")
"Publishers prefer to receive *loose* pages rather than three-ring binders."

lose (verb): to suffer the loss of (rhymes with "ooze")
"How did you *lose* so much money?" Crystal asked.

nauseated/nauseous

    nauseated: feeling sickness, or being queasy
        "Dorothy become *nauseated.*"

    nauseous: causing sickness
        "The fumes were *nauseous.*"

on to/onto

    on to (*on* is an adverb and *to* is a preposition)
        "We moved *on to* the next building."
    On modifies the verb *moved*—"*on*" is how we moved.
    To is the beginning of the prepositional phrase "*to* the next building."

    onto (preposition) means "to a position on."
Indicates that the subject is moving from one thing *to the top of* something else.
        "He helped her step *onto* the high platform."
        "The dog jumped *onto* the table."

oral/verbal

    oral: pertaining to the mouth
        "The medicine was administered *orally.*"

    verbal: associated with words or the process of putting ideas into words
        "The teacher gave the students *verbal* instructions."

passed/past

    passed (verb): past tense of *pass,* meaning "to move or go away"
        "The car *passed* us at sixty miles an hour."
        "Uncle Vincent *passed* away ten years ago."

    past (adjective): gone or elapsed
        "Your troubles are now *past.*"
    past (preposition): beyond
        "Jessica drove *past* the house."
    past (noun): a time gone by
        "Vickie regretted the *past.*"

peak/peek/pique

peak (noun): top, apex, or summit
"Pamela had reached the *peak* of her writing career."

peek (noun or verb): gander, glance, or glimpse
"She took a *peek* at Cal's manuscript after he *peeked* at hers."

pique (verb): to provoke, motivate, or stimulate
"The manuscript *piqued* the interest of several publishers."
pique (verb): to irritate, aggravate, or arouse anger or resentment
"What really *piques* editors is when writers use words improperly."
pique (noun): a transient feeling of wounded vanity
"In a fit of *pique,* she ripped the rejection letter into shreds."

personal/personnel

personal (adjective): relating to a person, or done in person
"This is a *personal* matter involving Judy and me."
"He conducted a *personal* interview."

personnel (noun): a group of persons (usually employed at the same place)
"The *personnel* in this office is very friendly." (Note: "a group" is singular, so use the singular verb form.)

pore/pour

pore (verb): to read seriously and intently (usually used with *over*)
"He found Liz in the den *poring* over the documents."

pour (verb): to cause to flow in a stream, or to dispense from a container
"Harry *poured* the coffee."
pour (verb): to give full expression to
"Fay *poured* out her feelings."
pour (verb): to rain hard
"It was *pouring* yesterday, but today is bright and sunny."

premier/premiere

premier (adjective): first in time (earliest), position, rank, or importance
"Bonnie's *premier* performance was in community theater."

premiere (noun): a first performance or exhibition
"The *premiere* of Abigail's play brought great reviews."
premiere (verb): to give a first public performance, or to appear for the first time as a star performer
"Bernadette *premiered* in Hamlet."

principal/principle

principal (noun): a chief person
"The *principal* of the school is a closet romance-novel reader."
principal (noun): a sum of money
"Try to pay off the *principal* of your loan, not just the interest."
principal (adjective): main, foremost, first, dominant, or leading
"His *principal* aim is to get published."

principle (always a noun): a guiding rule, a basic truth, or a doctrine
"That statement expresses a *principle* of modern physics."
"As a matter of *principle,* he refused to borrow money from anyone."

prophecy/prophesy

prophecy (noun): a prediction, foretelling, or revelation of things to come
"The *prophecy* has yet to be fulfilled." (Pronounced "pra-fe-SEE.")

prophesy (verb): to predict, to foretell, or to indicate what is to come
"What did the stranger *prophesy*?" (Pronounced "pra-fe-SIGH.")

Memory Device:
Pronounce the last syllable of the word *prophecy* and you will know it's spelled with a *c.*
A prophet might "sigh" when he *prophesies.*

raise/rise

raise (noun): addition or increase
"Aisha got a *raise* in her allowance."
raise (verb): to lift, uphold, resurrect, put up, build, or grow
"Did Jesus really *raise* Lazarus from the dead?"
"Yvonne *raised* cherry tomatoes in her garden."

NOTE: The verb *raise* is always transitive (needs an object).
"He *raised* his arm." (*Arm* is the object.)

rise (noun): an increase in amount, number, or volume
"Crime is on the *rise* in Los Angeles."
rise (verb): to assume an upright or standing position
"A gentleman should *rise* when a lady walks into the room."

NOTE: The verb *rise* is always intransitive.
"His arm *rises*." (His arm isn't rising *something*.)

reign/rein

reign (verb): to possess or exercise sovereign power; to rule
"The queen *reigned* over her royal subjects with a gentle hand."

rein (noun): a strap used to control an animal
rein (verb): to control, direct, check, or stop
"Connor *reined* in his stallion a few feet from Angela's mare by pulling on the *reins*."

set up/setup

set up (verb): to cause, create, bring about; to put in a compromising or dangerous position; to begin business
"Cathy *set up* shop just outside of town."

setup (noun): position, arrangement; something that has been constructed or contrived
"It was a perfect *setup*."

some time/sometime/sometimes

some time (*some* is an adjective; *time* is a noun)
"Lena and I spent *some time* together at the conference."

sometime (adverb): at some unspecified or unknown point in time (*at* is part of the definition)
"I went to that restaurant *sometime* last year."
"I'll do it *sometime* tomorrow."
sometime (adjective): occasional, or being such now and then
"She was a *sometime* opera singer."

sometimes (adverb): occasionally
"He visits me *sometimes*."

stationary/stationery

stationary (adjective): having a fixed or unmoving position, or not moving
"This huge rock is *stationary*."

stationery (noun): writing paper and envelopes, or office supplies
"This store's supply of *stationery* is almost exhausted."

Memory Device:
stationary means "st*a*nding" or "st*a*ying." (Note the *a*'s.)
stationery is used for writing l*e*tters with a p*e*n or p*e*ncil. (Note the *e*'s.)

their/there/they're

their (adjective): belonging to them
"Phoebe is *their* daughter."

there (adverb): in or at that place
"I was *there* when it happened."

they're is a contraction of "they are."
"We are disappointed because *they're* not going with us."

under way/underway

under way (adverb): in motion, or in progress
"The flight will be *under way* as soon as possible."

underway (adjective): occurring while traveling or in motion
"The fighter jet received an *underway* replenishment of fuel."

NOTE: It is usually preferable to replace "under way" with *begin* or *start*.
"The flight will begin as soon as possible."

verses/versus

verses (plural noun): poems or passages of Scripture

versus (preposition): against, in contrast to

waist/waste

waist (noun): midsection

waste (noun): trash, garbage, something expendable
waste (verb): to squander

whiskey/whisky

whiskey. If the liquor is made in the United States or Ireland, it's spelled with an *e.*

whisky. If it's from anywhere else, it's spelled without the *e.*

weather/whether

weather (noun) refers to atmospheric conditions.
  "The *weather* will be sunny and mild."

whether (conjunction) is used with stated or implied alternatives.
  "It's true, *whether* you like it or not!"

who's/whose

who's is a contraction for "who is" or "who has."
  "*Who's* going to write the next best seller?"
  "*Who's* been using my manuscript as a coloring book?"

whose (pronoun) is the possessive case of *who.*
  "*Whose* shoes are those?"
whose (adjective): of or relating to whom
  "She appealed to the editors, *whose* decisions were most important."

X-ray/Xray/x-ray

X-ray (noun): a radiation picture taken in a doctor's office
(Notice, capital *X* and hyphen. Webster's 10th did not have the hyphen.)
  "The doctor took an *X-ray.*"

Xray: communications code word for the letter *x.*
  "The policeman reported the license number as Alpha, Bravo, *Xray.*"

x-ray (verb): to examine, treat, or photograph with X-rays (Notice, small *x* and a hyphen)
  "The doctor *x-rayed* Sherry's ankle."

For Articles

The AP Stylebook has only one spelling for all forms of this word: *X-ray*.

---

your/you're

    your (adjective): of or relating to you
        "Is this *your* blouse?"

    you're: contraction for "you are"
        "*You're* the best!"

ADD YOUR OWN

My Most Confusing Words:

Word	Part of Speech	Definition

Word	Part of Speech	Definition

Section 3

Grammar

Entire books are written about all the facets of grammar, so I'll just touch on a few of
the most common mistakes and problems I've come across in my editing.

Common Grammatical Mistakes

among vs. between

Things are divided *between* two people or things, but *among* more than two. Thus, "The royalties will be divided equally *between* Mary, Beth and Connie" implies that the money is to be split into *two* equal portions. Mary gets half; Beth and Connie each receive a quarter. (The missing comma between Beth and Connie also supports the claim that Mary gets half while Beth and Connie split the other half.)

anxious vs. eager

anxious indicates fear, nervousness, extreme uneasiness, or worry (*anxiety*).
"Adriana was *anxious* about the exam."

eager means enthusiastic, ready to begin.
"Brooke was *eager* to start writing her new novel."

as vs. like

Use *as* when comparing phrases and clauses that contain a verb.
"Jeannie proofreads her work carefully *as* she should."

Use *like* to compare nouns and pronouns.
"Cristina writes *like* a pro."

couple vs. couple of

Use *couple* alone when used as a noun.
"Robert and Marcy made a cute *couple*."

When used as a modifier, add *of.*
It's never "a couple tomatoes." Always "a couple of tomatoes."

different from vs. different than

Things and people are *different from* each other.
"This guy is *different from* the other men I've met," Eileen said.
"Writing is *different from* speaking," Colleen said.

Different than is a convenient shortcut for "different from the way in which." In all but the most formal writing, *than* is preferable because it is shorter and tighter than "from the way in which." Example:
Today's style of writing is *different than* it was in C. S. Lewis's day.

each other vs. one another

Use *each other* when referring to two.
Angie and Alan discussed the book with *each other.*

Use *one another* when referring to more than two.
The critique group members discussed their manuscripts with *one another.*

fewer vs. less

Fewer refers to quantities/numbers.
"If you proofread your work carefully, you will get *fewer* rejections."

Less refers to amounts.
"First drafts require *less* work than rewrites."

lay vs. lie

Lay and *lie* are arguably the most difficult irregular verbs in the English language. The main confusion lies in the fact that while present-tense *lie* and present-tense *lay* mean two different things, the past tense of *lie* is *lay.* In addition, when people speak, these words are frequently misused, so our ears are used to hearing them incorrectly.

Lay (present tense): to put or place something or someone down
Lay is a "transitive verb," so it requires a direct object (the "something or someone").

Use present-tense *lay* when the action happens consistently or is happening presently.
"We *lay* our lives on the line for Christ every day."

The past tense of *lay* is *laid.*
> "Gwen *laid* her five-hundred-page manuscript on the bed."

The past-participle form of *lay* is *had laid.*
> "Athena *had laid* the last page of her manuscript on the table seconds before her three-year-old spilled the two-liter bottle of soda."

Other examples:
> "Carla *will lay* her notebook on the counter after she writes one hundred pages."
> "The dinner table *was laid* for six people."
> "*Laying* wallpaper is difficult work."

Lie (present tense): to rest or recline.
Lie is a state of being. It is an "intransitive verb," so no direct object follows. (Of course, there's another definition for *lie,* but it's not a problem word.)

Use present-tense *lie* when the action happens consistently or is happening presently.
> "Candy's dog *lies* on the guest bed every night."
> (The dog is resting/reclining. No action.)
> "Please *lie* down here."

The past tense of *lie* is *lay.*
> "Gloria *lay* in bed all night, dreaming of the day her novel would be published."

The past-participle form of *lie* is *has lain.*
> "Jill *has lain* in bed ever since her toddler spilled juice all over her manuscript."

Other examples:
> "The river *lies* between two hills; it has *lain* there for centuries."
> "The pen *is lying* on the desk."

more than vs. over
> *More than* is used with figures.
> "*More than* one thousand people bought Tim's book."
> "The grammar book has sold *more than* fifty thousand copies to date."

> *Over* refers to spatial relationships.
> "The football soared *over* the receiver's head."

Over can also be used with amounts.

"I paid *over* five dollars for that book."

(One could argue that the number of dollars you spent was more than five; however, here "five dollars" represents an *amount* of money.)

NOTE: Some references consider this an outdated distinction; others (including *The Associated Press Stylebook)* recommend following the traditional rule.

myriad

myriad (adjective): innumerable

"Louise looked at the *myriad* stars in the sky."

myriad (noun): a great number, or ten thousand

"They encountered *a myriad of* problems in their relationship."

"She experienced *myriads* of difficulties getting her book published."

NOTE: The noun usage of this word has been criticized in recent years, but Webster's 11th claims that it is acceptable.

reason, why, and because

reason (noun): explanation, justification, motive, or cause

why (noun, adverb, or conjunction): cause, reason, or purpose

because (conjunction): for the reason that

Correct examples:

"The *reason* Melanie writes fiction is *that* she loves reading it."

"I don't understand *why* more people don't read novellas."

"George writes nonfiction *because* he believes it helps people."

The following are incorrect:

"The *reason* Gwen writes fiction is *because* she loves reading it."

Here you'd be saying that the *reason* is *for the reason*.

"I don't understand the *reason why* more people don't read novellas."

You're saying you don't understand the *cause cause*.

"The *reason why* Tom writes nonfiction is *because* he believes it helps people."

Yikes! Here you're saying that the *cause cause* is *because*.

that vs. which

That is used with "restrictive clauses," phrases that narrow a category or identify a particular item in that category.

"Manuscripts *that* are not solicited by the publisher will be returned to sender."
In this example, the category is manuscripts. The "not solicited" phrase narrows the category to unsolicited manuscripts. If you took out the phrase, you'd have "Manuscripts will be returned to sender," which would be different.

Which is used with "nonrestrictive clauses," phrases that add something about an item already identified.

"My manuscript, *which* was not solicited by the publisher, was returned to me."
The item—"my manuscript"—is already identified. The "not solicited" phrase adds additional information. You could take out the phrase without changing the meaning of the sentence. "My manuscript was returned to me."

NOTE: *Which* clauses require commas; *that* clauses do not use commas.

that vs. who

That refers to animals and things.
"The dog *that* bit me chased the Frisbee *that* I threw."

Who refers to people.
"The man *who* bought Tammy flowers was handsome."

try and vs. try to

Try and should only be used when the subject is trying *and* doing something else.
"Three times Randy *tried and* failed to get his manuscript published."

Always use *try to* when referring to something the subject tried *to* accomplish.
"Ariana is going to *try to* write her first draft in a week."

was vs. were

The subjunctive mood (*were*) is used to express the following:

1. A condition contrary to fact
   "Oh, I wish I *were* an Oscar Mayer wiener."
   (Of course, I'm not. But that jingle will be stuck in your head all day now, won't it?)

2. A supposition
   "Suppose Marci *were* to arrive right now."

3. An improbable condition
   "Carrie drank the Pepsi as if there *were* no tomorrow. (Highly unlikely)

4. Uncertainty or doubt
   "If I *were* to marry you, how would you support me?" Irene asked.
   (There's uncertainty/doubt about whether she will marry him.)

5. Necessity
   "If it *were* absolutely necessary, I could rewrite my manuscript," David said.

6. A desire
   "Joan wishes she *were* going to the prom with Brandon."

ADD YOUR OWN

My Most Commonly Misused Words:

Word	Definition	Confusion

Word   Definition   Confusion

_____

_____

_____

_____

_____

_____

_____

_____

_____

_____

_____

_____

_____

_____

Modifiers

Dangling Modifiers

When you start a sentence with a modifying word or phrase, the subject of the sentence is what must be modified by that word or phrase. A "dangling modifier" is a phrase that does not clearly and sensibly modify the appropriate word. Examples:

"*Changing the oil every 3,000 miles, the Mustang* seemed to run better."
> A Mustang cannot change its own oil. So you'd want to rewrite that as something like:
> "Changing the oil every 3,000 miles, Fred found he got much better gas mileage."

"*Walking to work, the eucalyptus trees* reminded Lynette of Brandilyn Collins's latest novel."
> Eucalyptus trees don't walk to work…not even in Brandilyn's novels. So rewrite:
> "As Hope walked to work, the eucalyptus trees reminded her of *Eyes of Elisha.*"

"*Slamming on the brakes, the car* swerved off the road."
> Unless you're Stephen King, the car probably didn't slam on its own brakes. So:
> "Robin slammed on the brakes, and the car swerved off the road." Or:
> "When Robin slammed on the brakes, the car swerved off the road."

"*As a writer, words and punctuation* are the tools of your trade."
> "Words and punctuation" are not "a writer." So rewrite to something like this:
> "Words and punctuation are the writer's tools of the trade."

"Six months after attending Mount Hermon, Kim's article was accepted by a publisher."

"Kim's article" did not attend Mount Hermon. So rewrite to something like:

"Six months after Kim attended Mount Hermon, her article was accepted by a publisher."

Simultaneous Modifiers

Be sure the introductory phrase can be accomplished *at the same time as* the action in the rest of the sentence.

"Hugging the postman, Delilah ripped open the box containing her new novel."

Delilah cannot simultaneously hug the postman and rip open a box. Reword:

"After hugging the postman, Delilah ripped open the box containing her new novel."

Misplaced Modifiers

The position of a modifier determines what thing or action is being modified.

"Mona sent out a proposal for her book on living with horses last week."

Mona's proposal wasn't for a book about "living with horses last week." Reword:

"Last week Mona sent out a proposal for her book on living with horses."

"The editor told me on Thursday I have a book signing."

Did the editor say this on Thursday, or do you have a book signing on Thursday?

"On Thursday, the editor told me I have a book signing." Or:

"The editor told me I have a book signing on Thursday."

ADD YOUR OWN

Dangling or Misplaced Modifiers I've Caught in My Own (or Other Authors') Writing:

Phrase	Subject of Sentence	Suggested Rewrite

Phrase	Subject of Sentence	Suggested Rewrite

Pronouns

Pronoun/Antecedent Agreement

The *antecedent* is the noun to which a pronoun refers. The antecedent may appear in the same sentence as the pronoun or in an earlier one; occasionally, it comes after.

1. Make sure that every pronoun you use has an antecedent.
    "Amanda said she was going to the store." (*She* refers to *Amanda.*)

    Exception: The pronouns *it* and *who* can sometimes stand alone.
    "It's a beautiful day" or "It's going to rain."
    "Who was at the door?"

NOTE: Avoid using the stand-alone *it* as much as possible.

2. Don't start a new chapter or section with a pronoun. If you open with "He pulled out a gun and aimed it at her head," your reader will have no idea who these characters are. Chapter and section breaks often indicate a change in time, place, and/or point of view, so your reader cannot assume that the people referred to in the new chapter/section are the same ones talked about in the last one.

NOTE: If you're writing a suspense novel, you may want to keep the identity of a character a mystery. This is tricky, but can be done if you know what you're doing. Even so, it is better to use "the man" (or better yet, something more descriptive like "the handsome foreigner") instead of "he" at the beginning of a chapter or new section.

3. Don't confuse the reader with references that are unclear or ambiguous.
   "When Lori and Jan entered the room, Gayle noticed her right away."
   Which woman did Gayle notice?

4. Avoid using the word *it* in confusing contexts.
   "As Allison drove her car up to the service window, *it* made a rattling sound."
   Does *it* refer to the car or the window? Rewrite to something like:
   "As Allison drove up to the service window, her car made a rattling sound."

   "Audrey reached for her glass and drank it in one gulp."
   In this sentence, the *it* refers to the glass, and she didn't drink *the glass* in one gulp.

5. Make sure the pronoun and its antecedent agree in number.
   "Trevor's two sons are sloppy." (plural)
   "Neither *one of them* combs *his* hair." (singular)
   "Portia's two daughters are neat; *they* both clean up after *themselves*." (plural)

NOTE: In an effort to avoid gender bias (using *he* to refer to both sexes) and the annoying repetition of *him/her, he or she,* and the like, some people use *they* as a singular pronoun when referring to someone whose gender is unknown or irrelevant.
"If *an editor* (singular) likes your query, *they* (plural) will request a proposal."

However, using the plural pronoun *they* to refer to a singular antecedent presents a problem in agreement. This style is acceptable in verbal speech, but not in writing.

You could reword the above sentence to:
"If *an editor* likes your query, *he or she* will request a proposal." Or,
"If the *editors* like your query, *they* will request a proposal."

6. Most of the time, the subject pronoun of a phrase or sentence refers to the subject noun of the previous phrase or sentence, while the object pronoun refers to the object noun.
   "Stephanie told Nancy about the book signing. Then she told her about the potluck."
   ["She" refers to Stephanie (subject), and "her" refers to Nancy (object).]

   This rule of thumb does not apply if the identity of the pronoun is obvious.
   "Wanda told Daniel she wouldn't eat caviar. He told her he never ate shellfish."

Pronouns as Subjects or Objects

I, he/she, we, and *who* are subject pronouns. A subject is the one initiating something.

I like mystery novels.

He writes bestsellers.

She listens to opera.

We read nonfiction books.

Who reads historical romance?

Me, him/her, us, and *whom* are object pronouns. An object is the recipient of something.

Luke was talking to *me.*

Constance loves *him.*

Jason likes *her.*

Dad is taking *us* out to dinner.

To *whom* are you speaking?

Sounds easy, right? But it can get tricky when you have multiple people.

"Jeremy took Christine and I out to dinner" sounds right, but it's not.

I is a subject pronoun, not an object.

"Jeremy took Christine and me out to dinner" is correct.

How can you be sure? Take out the other person.

You wouldn't say, "Jeremy took I out to dinner."

The other time this is confusing is when the pronoun appears at the end of a sentence.

Is it "Joel writes better than *me*" or "Joel writes better than *I*"?

The trick here is to finish the thought. "Joel writes better than *I do.*"

When someone calls and asks to speak to Melinda, and you're Melinda, do you say, "This is her" or "This is she"?

The grammatically correct form is "This is she (who is speaking)."

Sounds pretty awkward, though, huh? You'd probably rather say, "This is Melinda."

The pronouns *who* and *whom* can be confusing. But there are some tricks you can use with these too.

1. Try substituting a he/she or him/her pronoun. If he/she fits, use *who*. If him/her fits, use *whom*.

   Marty, *who* rented the room, left the window open. (*He* rented the room.)

   Marty, to *whom* the room was rented, left the window open. (It was rented to *him*.)

2. *whom* is always preceded by a preposition because the action has to happen *to, with,* or *for* the person being referred to.

   The man *to whom* you wrote the check no longer works at this company.

   The bowlers *with whom* I play won every tournament last season.

   The audience *for whom* the book was written is teenage girls.

ADD YOUR OWN

My Worst Pronoun/Antecedent Problems:

_____

_____

_____

_____

_____

_____

_____

_____

Subject/Verb Agreement

Make sure the subject and the verb agree in number (singular or plural).

"The synopsis and sample chapter (two things) *have* to be mailed by Tuesday."

"Each proposal (singular) *has* to be mailed separately."

"Every contest entry (singular) *has* to be received before the deadline."

"None (*not one,* singular) of the stories in that book *is* written in present tense."

When a subject is followed by a phrase that refers to another entity (with or without commas), the added phrase does not change the quantity of the original subject.

"Terry's bad grammar, as well as her typos, *needs* to be corrected."

"The suspenseful plot combined with unexpected twists *makes* this a great book."

Some collective nouns can be treated as either plural or singular, depending on whether you want the focus to be on the unit or on the individual members.

"The couple *has* a young daughter." (refers to the two people as a single unit)

"The couple *get* along well together." (focus is on two individuals, plural "they")

"My family *is* very close." (focus is on the unit, which is singular)

"My family *want* the best for me." (reference is to several people, plural "they")

ADD YOUR OWN

My Worst Subject/Verb Problems:

_____

_____

_____

_____

_____

My Worst Pronoun Problems:

_____

_____

_____

_____

_____

_____

_____

_____

_____

_____

_____

_____

Grammar Myths

Generations of English teachers have taught students certain rules that are either personal preferences or rules that have changed over time.

Myth #1. Never split an infinitive. (See *CMOS* 5.160.)

An *infinitive* is the *to* form of a verb: to go, to holler, to whisper, to study. *Splitting an infinitive* means to put some word (usually an adverb) between the *to* and the verb: to *quickly* go, to *loudly* holler, to *quietly* whisper, to *avidly* study.

Rule of thumb: If it's just as easy to word something in a way that avoids splitting an infinitive, do so—if for no better reason than because some readers, editors, and proofreaders will fault you if you don't. However, if doing so interrupts the flow, or makes comprehension difficult, go ahead and split that infinitive.

Myth #2. Never start a sentence with a conjunction. (See *CMOS* 5.191.)

A *conjunction* is a word that defines the relationship between different units of thought. Examples: *and, so, but, if, or.* Writers are often taught that beginning a sentence with a conjunction makes it incomplete, a sentence fragment. And sometimes that's true.

Example: "Try to catch me. If you can."

But sentence fragments are perfectly acceptable (if not overused, confusing, or unclear). Experienced writers may deliberately use the occasional sentence fragment for emphasis or to create a particular tone. (Note, however, that a dash can also be used for emphasis, and it is preferable if the effect is the same.)

In many cases, opening with a conjunction does *not* turn a sentence into a fragment; it simply serves to connect the current information more strongly to the information that comes before it. Beginning a sentence with a conjunction is sometimes the best way to express the sentence's relationship with the previous one. As with sentence fragments, avoid overdoing this type of sentence construction.

Myth #3. Never end a sentence with a preposition. (See *CMOS* 5.169.)

A *preposition* is a word that combines with a noun phrase to form a modifying phrase. Most prepositions refer to time, space, or position. Examples:

across the country	*after* the movie
at the store	*in* the room
with ketchup	

Many students are taught that prepositions should never come at the end of a sentence. However, the proper ordering of prepositions can sometimes result in sentences that sound awkward, stilted, or pompous.

As a general rule, try to avoid ending sentences with prepositions. But if that's the only way to avoid sounding awkward, then by all means, break the rule. Sometimes a preposition is the best word to end a sentence *with*.

Myth #4. Never use the word *hopefully* in place of "It is hoped" or "I/we hope."

Many writers have been upbraided in recent years for using what is sometimes considered the colloquial usage of this word. The argument is that *hopefully* means "in a hopeful manner." Therefore, a sentence like "Hopefully this will clear things up" could only mean "This will clear things up *in a hopeful manner*."

However, according to the latest edition of *Merriam-Webster's Collegiate Dictionary*, *hopefully* has two meanings. #1 is "in a hopeful manner." #2 is "It is hoped; I hope; we hope." The example given is "Hopefully the rain will end soon."

Webster's further explains that this second definition of *hopefully* is in a class of adverbs known as disjuncts. Disjuncts are a way for the author (or speaker) to comment directly to the reader (or hearer) based on the content of the sentence. Many other adverbs (*interestingly, frankly, clearly, luckily, unfortunately*) are similarly used. Webster's states that the second definition of *hopefully* is "entirely standard."

BONUS TIP

When you write dialogue, you can choose to ignore a lot of these grammar rules. The way people talk is often quite different from the way they speak. As a matter of fact, you might *want* to write certain characters with specific grammatical habits that give the reader insight into their personalities or to identify a character's unique voice. (You probably wouldn't, for example, have a teenager or a country bumpkin or an old-timer or an uneducated farm boy using impeccable grammar...unless there's something special about that character, like his mother is a professional author!)

Even well-educated people often break grammar rules in speech. Most of us use pronouns, for example, based on whether they "sound right." Using the correct pronoun can sometimes make people sound arrogant, as if they are putting on airs. (For example, "To whom do you wish to speak?" is proper, but "Who do you want to talk to?" sounds more natural.)

The trick: Know what the grammar rules are, and only break a rule if you are doing so intentionally with a specific purpose in mind.

Section 4

Spelling

The most important advice I can give you about spelling is this:

Do Not Rely on Spell Check!

There are too many mistakes it won't catch, such as "real words" that are not used properly in context. In addition, no spell-check software will have all the spellings in the latest edition of the appropriate dictionary (*Merriam-Webster's Collegiate* for books; *Webster's New World College Dictionary* for articles).

Any word you are unsure of should be looked up. I would advise keeping a list of your own "commonly misspelled words" on a computer file or in this book.

To get you started, here are a few misspelled words I come across often in my editing. Most are "everyday" words, the kind of things you might not think to look up.

Commonly Misspelled Words

a lot (two words)

acknowledgment (not *acknowledgement)*

air-condition (verb)
air conditioner (noun—notice, no hyphen)
air-conditioning (noun)
air-conditioned (adjective)

airfare (one word)

airmail (one word)

all right

Although most dictionaries list *alright* as a legitimate word, most book publishers do not consider it acceptable. *The AP Stylebook* says never to use *alright.* (See page 12.)

Webster's Collegiate says that since the early twentieth century some critics have insisted *alright* is wrong, though it has its defenders and users.

Many readers today consider *alright* to be wrong, but no one has a problem with *all right.* So I would personally recommend avoiding the one-word spelling.

babysit/babysat/babysitting/babysitter

One word (no hyphen) according to Webster's Collegiate.

For Articles

According to *The AP Stylebook* (p. 25), should be *baby-sit, baby-sitting, baby-sat* (one word with a hyphen), but *baby sitter* (two words, no hyphen).

backyard
Spell as one word, whether used as a noun or adjective.

How's this for confusing?

According to *The AP Stylebook* (p. 25), spell this as one word (*backyard*) when used as an adjective, two words (*back yard*) when used as a noun.

However, *Webster's New World College Dictionary*, which *The AP Stylebook* recommends, has the *exact opposite*: one word (*backyard*) when used as a noun, two words (*back yard*) when used as an adjective.

barbed wire (not *barb wire*)

bookstore (one word)

brainpower (one word, not two)

brussels sprout (not *brussel sprouts* or *Brussels sprouts*)

by-product (with a hyphen)

cannot (one word, not two)

CAT scan (all-caps CAT, acronym for Computerized Axial Tomography)

deathbed (one word, not two)

dining (I see this spelled with two *n*'s all the time, probably because *dinning* is also a word, so spell check doesn't catch it.)

divorcé (a divorced man)
divorcée (a divorced woman)

espresso (not *expresso*)

fiancé (a man engaged to be married)
fiancée (a woman engaged to be married)

For Articles

The AP Stylebook (p. 94) does not use accent marks over the *e*'s in fiance and fiancee.

freelance/freelancer/freelancing (no hyphen)

good-bye (with a hyphen and an *e*)

For Articles

According to *The AP Stylebook* (p. 106), spell as one word, *goodbye*, without a hyphen.

good night (two words, no hyphen)

grown-up (with a hyphen, both noun and adjective)

handheld (one word, no hyphen)

> # For Articles
>
> According to *The AP Stylebook* (p. 111), use a hyphen: *hand-held*.

handmade (one word, no hyphen)

harebrained (not *hairbrained*)

homemade (one word, no hyphen)

iced tea (not *ice tea*)

insofar as

ma'am

makeup (no hyphen)

man-made (with a hyphen)

millennium (two *l*'s and two *n*'s)

mind-set (notice the hyphen)

monthlong (adjective, no hyphen)

nationwide (no hyphen)

newsstand (one word, no hyphen)

oceangoing (one word, no hyphen)

old-fashioned (not *old fashion*, and always with a hyphen)

oohed/oohing and *aahed/aahing* (notice the double-a)

predominant/predominantly (preferred over *predominate* and *predominately*)

restaurateur (not *restauranteur*)

Smithsonian Institution (not *Smithsonian Institute*)

straitjacket (not *straight-jacket*)

T-shirt (with a capital *T* and a hyphen)

well-being

Whenever two spellings are given in the dictionary, the first one listed is the preferred spelling. For example:
> *amid* (not *amidst*)
> *among* (not *amongst*)
> *backward* (not *backwards*)
> *forward* (not *forwards*)
> *gray* (not *grey*)
> *till* (not *'til*)
> *toward* (not *towards*)

Even the Reference Books Sometimes Disagree

Occasionally there is a discrepancy between reference books. For example, *Webster's Collegiate Dictionary* (11ᵗʰ edition) says that **coworker** should be spelled without a hyphen. *The Chicago Manual of Style* (15ᵗʰ edition) says that it "conforms largely" to *Merriam-Webster's Collegiate Dictionary*. However, while it lists closed spellings for *coequal, coauthor,* and *coeditor,* it hyphenates **co-worker**.

Though *The Chicago Manual of Style* is above *Webster's* on the priority scale for most book publishers, since *CMOS* did not specify **co-worker** with a hyphen in the 14ᵗʰ edition, I suspect most publishers will stick with Webster's unhyphenated spelling, **coworker**.

For Articles

The Associated Press Stylebook suggests retaining the hyphen for "co-" words that indicate occupation or status, such as ***co-author, co-host, co-owner, co-partner, co-pilot, co-signer, co-star,*** and ***co-worker.*** However, this is an exception to their own *Webster's New World College Dictionary.*

INTERESTING QUOTE

Many cultures believed the letters of their alphabets were far more than just symbols for communication, recording transactions, or recalling history. They believed letters were powerful magical symbols that could be used to cast spells and predict the future. The Norse runes and the Hebrew alphabet are simple letters for spelling words, but also deep symbols of cosmic significance. This magical sense is preserved in our word *spelling.* When you "spell" a word correctly, you are in effect casting a spell, charging these abstract, arbitrary symbols with meaning and power.

—from *The Writer's Journey* by Christopher Vogler

Trademarks

⟿⧽⊙

Many generic-sounding words and phrases are actually trademarked brand names. Trademarked words aren't off-limits for writers, but be sure to double-check the spelling and use proper capitalization. If a general term is sufficient, use it instead of the product name. Some words are legally restricted. (See the International Trademark Association, www.inta.org, for a list.)

Here are a few examples:

Band-Aid (with a hyphen, capital *A*; generic: adhesive bandage)
Bubble Wrap (generic: air-filled plastic packaging material)
ChapStick (one word, with a capital *S*)
Coke (generic: cola, soda, or pop, depending on the area of the country)
Crock-Pot (with a hyphen, capital *P*)
Dumpster (generic: trash bin, trash receptacle, trash container, etc.)
Frisbee (generic: toy flying saucer)
Hula-Hoop (with a hyphen, capital *H*; generic: plastic toy hoop)
Jacuzzi (generic: whirlpool, spa, therapeutic whirlpool bath)
Jell-O (with a hyphen and a capital *O*; generic: gelatin or pudding)
Jet Ski (generic: personal watercraft, recreational watercraft)
Jaws of Life (tool to pry open a vehicle to free people trapped inside)
Jetway (passenger ramp between a terminal building and an aircraft)
Kmart (no hyphen, no space, lowercase *m*)
Kitty Litter (generic: cat box filler)
Kleenex (generic: tissue)
La-Z-Boy (with two hyphens, capital *Z* and *B*; generic: recliner, chair and ottoman)

LEGO (all caps)
Laundromat (generic: self-service laundry)
Ping-Pong (two capital Ps and a hyphen, except when used generically for bouncing)
Post-it Note (capitalize *post* and *note,* but not *it.* Hyphenate.)
Q-Tip (with a hyphen, capital *T*; generic: cotton swab)
Scotch tape (generic: adhesive tape)
Silly Putty (generic: modeling clay)
Styrofoam (thick material insulated cups are made from)
Teflon (nonstick coating)
Wal-Mart (with a hyphen, capital *M*)
Windbreaker (generic: lightweight jacket)
Xerox (photocopier, printer, copier, scanner)

NOTE: Trademark symbols (® and ™) are not used in fiction. For nonfiction, many publishers use them the first time each product is mentioned, but not thereafter. Be sure to determine whether the name is a registered trademark (®) or not (™).

ADD YOUR OWN

My Most Commonly Misspelled Words:

How I Usually Spell It   How It Should Be Spelled

_____   _____

_____   _____

_____   _____

_____   _____

_____   _____

_____   _____

How I Usually Spell It   How It Should Be Spelled

Publishers' Preferences

Each publisher will have its own list of preferences. Until you've started working for a specific house, follow the above-referenced resources. Occasionally, however, you'll come across an instance where the industry-standard guidelines differ from one book to the next. Here's one example.

OK vs. ***okay*** vs. ***ok***

Merriam-Webster's Collegiate Dictionary lists *OK* as the standard spelling, with *okay* as a "variant." (Probably because "OK" was originally an abbreviation of *oll korrect*, a facetious alteration of *all correct*, back in 1839.)

Most book publishers seem to prefer *okay*. But one publisher I've worked with likes *OK*. So if you're working with a particular house, ask what their preference is. If not, either one is . . . acceptable.

Since more publishers seem to like *okay*, that's what I use (except when I'm sending something to a publisher whose known preference is *OK*).

For Articles

The AP Stylebook says to always use *OK,* not *okay.*

Just never, *ever,* use "*ok,*" okay?

Terms for Modern Technology

The Internet has been around for a while now. But it's new enough that the "experts" haven't figured out how to spell words associated with it. For example, Webster's 10th edition had E-mail (capitalized) as a noun, but e-mail (lowercase) as a verb. The 11th edition lists the lowercase form for both (but always hyphenated, contrary to what you see used a lot). The 10th edition hyphenated on-line. The 11th edition doesn't.

Here's what the 11th edition of *Merriam-Webster's Collegiate Dictionary* and *The AP Stylebook* have:

Internet (always capitalized)

e-mail (lowercase, hyphenated)

online (lowercase, no hyphen)
 one word when used as an adjective or adverb
  "an *online* database" "I'm *online* shopping right now"

 two words when used as a noun phrase
  "I am *on line* with the editor right now."
  "Put me *on line* with the president."
  "If you can get my computer back *on line*, I'll send you a box of chocolates!"

Web site (two words; capitalize Web but not site)
 but ***webcam, webcast,*** and ***webmaster*** are one word, listed as "often capped"

For Articles

Webster's New World College Dictionary has *website* as the primary spelling, with *web site* and *Web site* as alternates.

NOTE: Dictionaries occasionally change spellings with new editions, especially with technology terms. So make sure you're using the most updated version.

ADD YOUR OWN

Favorite Modern-Technology Terms:

_____

_____

_____

_____

_____

_____

_____

_____

_____

Slang/Sounds

Some slang words and sound words are listed in the dictionary, so always look these words up. Here are some examples:

c'mon: abbreviation for "come on."
> "*C'mon*, Ruth," Ann pleaded. "Let's call Carolyn right now and give her the news."

NOTE: This word is listed in *Webster's New World College Dictionary* (for articles) but *not* in *Webster's Collegiate Dictionary* (for books). However, even in books, it is a commonly accepted contraction.

huh: used to express surprise, disbelief, or confusion; or as an inquiry inviting affirmative reply
> "*Huh*," Wayne said as he stared at the confusing lesson in Kathy's workbook.
> "*Huh!*" Gordon mumbled. "I never knew about that spelling rule."
> "*Huh?*" Cari asked, certain she couldn't possibly have heard Deborah correctly.

li'l: abbreviation for "little"

sh: used to urge or command silence or less noise (Webster's 11th says the pronunciation is "often prolonged," so no need to add more *h*'s.)
> "*Sh*," Miranda cautioned. "Alexander's in the next room!"

uh-huh: used to indicate affirmation, agreement, or gratification (slang for "yes")
> "*Uh-huh*," Dustin said, nodding. "You heard what I said."

uh-uh: used to indicate negation (slang for "no")

"*Uh-uh,*" Max replied. "I will not do that, no matter what Edwina said."

wannabe

A person who aspires to be someone or something else or who tries to look or act like someone else. (Plural: *wannabes.*)

"She wrote like a Danielle Steele *wannabe.*"

NOTE: Webster's 10th spelled this with a hyphen: *wanna-be.*

y'all (not "yawl" or "ya'll")

Variant of "you all."

"*Y'all* want to watch *Gone With the Wind* tonight?" Joyce asked.

yea (pronounced "yay")

A cheer, like "Hurray!"

yeah

colloquial form of *yes*

"Well, *yeah,* of course I love you," Gene told Lizzy.

ADD YOUR OWN

My Favorite Slang/Sound Words:

How Webster's Spells It   Definition

_____

_____

_____

_____

Hyphenation

The Chicago Manual of Style contains an extensive guide (#7.90) for determining when certain words should be spelled with a hyphen. In many cases, you can consult Webster's 11th to see if a hyphen is used in the spelling of a compound word or if it should be spelled as one word. Here are some examples based on the *CMOS* list:

Ages

Though *CMOS*-14 differentiated between hyphenated spellings for nouns and adjectives, *CMOS*-15 recommends hyphenating both.

"My ten-year-old is taking swimming lessons from a seventeen-year-old girl."

For Articles

The AP Stylebook (pp. 8–9) also suggests using hyphens with ages for both compound nouns and adjectives.

Colors

Color-term compounds in which one word modifies another are not hyphenated.

"sea green"   "greenish blue"   "jet black"

Exception: "established expressions" are hyphenated before a noun but not after.
"The truth isn't always black and white" but "a black-and-white print"

If two colors in a compound are of equal importance, the compound is hyphenated.
"blue-gray sky"   "red-green colorblindness"

If two or more words denote a blend of colors, the compound is hyphenated before a noun, not hyphenated after the noun.
"His cheek was black and blue"   "a black-and-blue cheek"

A bouquet of "red and white roses" would consist of some red roses and some white roses. If each rose has both colors in it, you'd have a bouquet of "red-and-white roses."

Compound Modifiers, *CMOS* #5.92–5.93, 7.86, 7.90 and *AP* p. 333
Many modifying phrases are hyphenated when followed by the noun the phrase describes, but not hyphenated if the phrase follows the noun it describes (unless there's a risk of ambiguity or misunderstanding).

Adjective + Adjective
"The stove was red hot" but "a red-hot stove" (unless the stove was both hot and red, in which case you would write "a red, hot stove" or "a hot, red stove")

Adjective + Noun (or Noun + Adjective)
"The manuscript was high quality"   "a high-quality manuscript"
"Writing a novel is time consuming"   "a time-consuming project"
"This computer is user friendly"   "a user-friendly software program"

Adjective + Participle
"The question was open ended"   "an open-ended question"

Noun + Gerund *(a noun that expresses generalized or uncompleted action)*
"fiction writing"   "a fiction-writing clinic"

Noun + Participle
"The novel was suspense filled"   "a suspense-filled novel"

Number + Superlative
"His book was fourth to last in the contest"   "the fourth-to-last contestant"
"The spine is three inches thick"   "a three-inch-thick spine"

Participle + Noun
"Their manuscript was on the cutting edge"   "cutting-edge technology"

Participle + Preposition
"This poem is often quoted"   "an often-quoted poem"

Multiple-Word Modifiers
"twentieth-century near-future speculative fiction"
"twenty-four-hour-a-day schedule"

If two adjective phrases end in a common noun, use a hyphen after each of the unattached words to show that they are both related to the noun.
"This year's schedule includes several three- and four-day clinics."
"This book is targeted for four- to six-year-old children."

Potential Misreading
Occasionally, you may run into a situation where a compound adjective that follows the noun might lead to confusion or ambiguity. For example, "Maureen's book was thought provoking" could mean that her book provoked thought or that it was thought (considered) to be provoking. If a potential for misreading exists (or the possibility of a distracting, even humorous, secondary interpretation), use a hyphen.
Other examples:
much-loved music ("much loved music" could refer to a lot of loved music)
less-appreciated art ("less appreciated art" could mean fewer appreciated sketches)

Adverb Phrases, *CMOS* #5.93, 7.87, 7.90 and *AP* p. 152
Phrases that include an *-ly* adverb are not hyphenated.
"a mildly worded rejection letter"   "Amelia's novel has a highly developed plot."
"Vanessa's heroine felt utterly dejected when Roger left her at the altar."

Exception: Hyphenate if the adverb is part of an adjective phrase.
"a not-so-mildly-worded rejection letter"

Adverb phrases that do *not* end in *-ly* are hyphenated before but not after a noun.

"Her book was much loved"   "a much-loved book"
"The man was well read"   "a well-read man"

Exception: compounds with *most* and *least* are usually open.

"Some of the least skilled writers in the county entered that contest."

Exception: Check Webster's for compound words that are always hyphenated, no matter what their usage. For example:

"Peggy's husband was long-suffering."
"Had Jayna been a long-suffering wife for too many years?"
"Christ exhibited a spirit of long-suffering we should all emulate."

Prefixes and Suffixes

The Chicago Manual of Style has a great chart (#7.90) that lists prefixes and suffixes that are commonly combined with other words, and indicates which ones are open, which are hyphenated, and which are closed. Here are a few examples:

all

Most adjective compounds with *all* are hyphenated.

all-inclusive   all-around   all-powerful

Most adverb compounds with *all* are not hyphenated.

all along   all in   all over

Some depend on whether they come before or after a noun.

"She went all out" but "an all-out war"

cross

Most compounds with *cross* are hyphenated; a few are closed.
If not listed in a dictionary, the compound should be hyphenated.

cross-referenced   cross-country
crosstown   crosscut   crossover

full

All compound adjectives with *full* are hyphenated before a noun, but not hyphenated after the noun.

> full-length mirror, full-scale drawing, full-time job
> Annabel's mirror is full length.
> Marcia's drawing is full scale.
> Cynthia's job is full time.

like

The suffix *like* is often used to form new compounds. These are usually closed except for words ending in *l* or *ll*, words of three or more syllables, compound words, most proper nouns, or other forms that might be difficult to read. When in doubt, hyphenate.

> childlike
> sail-like, vacuum-bottle-like
> Whitman-like, but Christlike

over, under

Adjectives with the prefix *over* or *under* are closed unless they are multiple-word modifiers containing *the*, in which case they are hyphenated.

> overexposed, overrated, underhanded
> over-the-counter, under-the-table

self

Most adjectives with *self* and another word are hyphenated. When the additional prefix *un* is used, close the compound. When *self* is added to a suffix, the word is closed.

> self-reliant, self-sustaining, self-righteous, self-confident, self-conscious
> unselfconscious
> selfless, selfish

well, ill, better, best, little, lesser, and *least* **with an adjective or participle**

Compounds with these words are hyphenated before the noun, open after a noun, and open if modified by an adverb.

> "He was well known"   "a well-known author"   "a very well known writer"
> "She was better prepared for her second meeting with the publisher than she was the first time."
> "She's a better-prepared writer."
> "I was much better prepared."

ADD YOUR OWN

My Most Confusing Compound Words:

<u>Correct Spelling</u>   <u>Definition/Usage</u>

_____

_____

_____

_____

_____

_____

_____

_____

_____

_____

_____

_____

Numbers

Simple Fractions (see *CMOS* #9.15)
Hyphenate spelled-out fractions (except when the second part is already hyphenated).
one-half   three-quarters   a two-thirds majority
one and three-quarters   three fifty-thirds

Mixed Fractions (see *CMOS* #9.16)
Don't join whole numbers to fractions with hyphens.
"Niki's manuscript was four and one-eighth inches thick."
"She wrote for twenty-one and one-quarter hours straight."
"His second book was two and three-quarters as long as his first one."

Fractions as Compound Modifiers
Hyphenate fractions when they're used as adjectives, but not when they're used as nouns.
"Clarissa wrote for a half hour. After her half-hour session, she ate chocolate cake."

Measurements
Adjective compounds that have a number and a unit of measure are hyphenated when they come before a noun.
"Laura jogged a three-mile path."
"Gary's car left a 150-yard skid mark."

When an adjective is added after the unit of measure, the adjective and the unit are joined by a hyphen.

"Flavia bought a two-year-old car."
"Cecilia's teacher is a sixty-five-year-old man."
"Jay babysat a two-and-a-half-year-old child."
"Patricia has twin six-year-old girls."
"Cliff's son scaled a three-meter-high wall."

When the compound adjective is preceded by another modifying number, the hyphenated compound is kept separate from that number.

"Brian's class consisted of twenty-four five-year-old boys."
"Margo's dogs drink two three-ounce bottles of water every day."

If the compound comes after the noun, it may be left open.

"Brent met a man sixty-five years old."
"Paula's niece is two and a half years old."
"Penelope climbed a wall three meters high."
"Charlie's son had a party with twenty-four boys five years old."

When numerals are used and the units are abbreviated, don't use a hyphen even before the noun.

33 m distance   12 kg weight   3 m high wall   3 ft. high wall   1200 lb. stone

ADD YOUR OWN

My Favorite Numbers Rules:

_____

_____

_____

_____

_____

_____

My Favorite Miscellaneous Spelling Rules:

_____

_____

_____

_____

_____

_____

_____

_____

_____

_____

_____

_____

_____

My Favorite Miscellaneous PUGS Rules:

_____

_____

_____

_____

_____

_____

_____

_____

_____

_____

_____

_____

_____

Conclusion

I hope you enjoy *Polishing the "PUGS."* Additional copies are available through my Web site, www.KathyIde.com, or by sending me an e-mail request at Kathy@KathyIde.com.

I am also available to speak at writers' conferences on this topic (and others).

If you've studied these guidelines and feel you'd like to have some one-on-one, hands-on help with your manuscript (or even just a few chapters of it), please e-mail me. I edit all levels of writing, from first-time, never-before-published authors through the final proofing stage before a manuscript is published. I offer a $5/hour discount on my standard hourly rate to anyone who has purchased this book.

Kathy Ide
Author/Ghostwriter
Editor/Mentor
Writers' Conference Speaker
Editor Services Coordinator

Kathy@KathyIde.com
www.KathyIde.com

Printed in the United States
89506LV00004B/19-26/A

9 781414 110318